GROWING VEGETABLES
IN THE PACIFIC NORTHWEST

Illustrated by Drew M. Elicker

MADRONA PUBLISHERS, INC. • SEATTLE

GROWING

VEGETABLES

IN THE

PACIFIC

NORTHWEST

JILL SEVERN

Library of Congress Cataloging in Publication Data

Severn, Jill, 1947-
  Growing vegetables in the Pacific Northwest.

  Includes index.
  1. Vegetable gardening—Northwest, Pacific.
I. Title.
SB321.S48   635'.09795   77-29260
ISBN 0-914842-25-0

Published simultaneously in Canada as *Growing Vegetables:*
A Guide for the Pacific Gardener
ISBN 0-88894-171-4

USA   CANADA
Madrona Publishers, Inc.   Douglas & McIntyre Ltd.
113 Madrona Place East   1875 Welch Street
Seattle, Washington 98112   North Vancouver, B.C.

For Mom,

my favorite hardy perennial

Acknowledgments

My thanks must first go to my neighbor, Gail Smith, who taught me the rudiments of gardening and the value of horse manure. Another gardener, Myrtle James, who grows more vegetables in less space than anyone I know, also deserves special thanks for her contribution of ideas and encouragement and for her careful reading of the manuscript. And it is to Cathy Rogers that I owe my gratitude for introducing me to the wonders of artichoke growing.

If thanks were money, my mother would be a very wealthy woman; it was she who typed most of the manuscript for this little opus, and it is her unerring grammatical sense that is responsible for some of the better sentences in it.

To my husband Jack, son Joshua, and brother-in-law David I am also grateful. Their patience, help, and support have been invaluable.

And finally, justice dictates that lightning should strike me where I sit were I not to thank Dan Levant of Madrona Publishers, the avuncular muse of this entire proceeding.

J.S.

Acknowledgments

The illustrator acknowledges the cooperation and encouragement of the friends and neighbors who opened their homes and gardens to him. Special thanks must go to Glen Ison of Port Townsend for many pleasant hours sketching in his magnificent garden.

D. M. E.

Contents

[ix]

Part One

Initial Investments

The difference between success and failure in the vegetable garden has nothing to do with the color of your thumbs. The real key to an orderly, productive, and satisfying garden depends, more than anything else, on the amount of time that is devoted to its care.

An almost universal fault of first-time gardeners is to plant more than they can take care of, and probably nothing I can say will change that. I would, however, like to encourage new gardeners to think about just what they are getting into when they first plunge their shovels into the earth.

Vegetable gardens, like children and milk cows, cannot be left unattended for very long. In the early part of the season, when tender young plants are just coming out of the ground, a garden needs daily attention. Seeds must be watered daily to germinate; young plants must be watched carefully and protected from marauding slugs and insects. You cannot plant seeds and then leave for a three-week vacation.

When your peas begin to bear, they will need to be picked once every three or four days, and, at the same time, the tomatoes will need to be tied to their stakes, the lettuce will need to be thinned, and the weeds will threaten to take over if you're not there to pull them.

[3]

If this begins to sound like slavery to you, you have just learned an important lesson of gardening.

If you are a new vegetable gardener starting a garden in land that hasn't been gardened before, even more consideration should be given to the extent of your commitment. New land requires special preparation: there may be brush to clear or sod to remove, and there will probably be rocks to haul out and manure or compost to dig in. How much time it takes just to prepare the ground will vary, depending on the condition of the earth you start with, the condition of your body, and how much previous practice you've had wielding a shovel. All of these things will become easier with each passing year, of course; the condition of your soil will improve, as will the condition of your body and your dexterity with the tools of the trade.

So how much land should you start with? For someone who's never tended more than a few houseplants, I would probably recommend a plot no bigger than fifteen feet square. The decision of how much land to till is entirely your own, but for the inexperienced and the busy, starting small is best.

This decision may, of course, be governed by the amount of suitable land you have available; if you live in an apartment and will be gardening in containers on your balcony, or if you have only a small yard in the city, you will be spared some decision-making.

In addition to your investment of space and time, you will need to make an investment in gardening tools if you don't already have them.

There are hundreds of gardening gadgets on the market, most of which aren't really necessary, and some of which are downright useless. Only a few are really essential: a good shovel, a strong metal rake, and a hand trowel. A sturdy

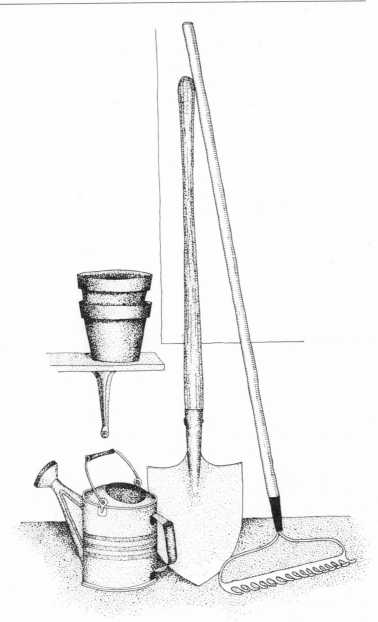

shovel is essential for preparing the ground, digging in compost and manure, and for leaning on. A strong metal rake will break up clumps of earth, rake out roots and debris, and make furrows for planting seeds in. A trowel is essential for transplanting young seedlings and setting out bedding plants.

Some gardeners would add a hoe to this list for weeding, but I rarely use one, since I find it more effective to pull weeds by hand than to beat them to death with a hoe.

A pitchfork is also handy for shoveling manure and compost, and a couple of buckets are useful for carrying fertilizer and lime, and for mixing fish fertilizer and manure tea.

If your plot is very large, you may want to consider buying a rototiller, a small plough that looks like an overgrown lawnmower. This investment is a large one, however, and probably ought to wait a year or two until you've decided whether gardening is really a life-long commitment for you. If your plot is too large to dig by hand, it is generally fairly inexpensive to hire someone with a rototiller to plough it for you or to rent a rototiller and till it yourself.

A good garden hose equipped with an adjustable nozzle that allows you to make a fine, gentle spray for tender, young seedlings is also an essential item.

Nothing is more wasteful than buying poorly made tools and equipment. I have yet to find a use for a bent trowel, a shovel with a broken handle, or a hose that leaks. And there is great pleasure in owning well-made tools that you will use year after year, until they become old friends. Buy the best, treat them well, and you will be money ahead. Rakes, shovels, and other metal tools should be cleaned and oiled several times a year, and should never be left out in the rain. Garden hose should be drained and put away at the end of the gardening season. Respect for one's tools is always the sign of a good craftsman.

And a few words should be said about the seeds and plants you will be buying. There is a rather large industry devoted to supplying the home gardener with seeds, plants, tools, insecticides, fertilizers, and yes, steer manure, in both its literal and its figurative forms. You can buy both seeds and plants from seed catalogues and avoid the impulse buying that sometimes takes place when you go to a nursery, but sooner or later you will need something—probably many things— that are best purchased from your nearby nursery or garden store. For the first-time gardener, walking into a nursery can seem like visiting a foreign country. You ask for fertilizer for your petunias, and the clerk says, "Do you want to make them grow or to make them bloom?" You would like to inquire about the difference between the two, but there are six people waiting in line behind you, and you suddenly feel inexcusably ignorant. "Grow," you blurt, and go out wondering why you can't have something that will make your petunias grow and bloom too.

The first and most important way to avoid such scenes is to refrain from going to garden stores on weekends when the people there will be too busy to talk to you. Choose a nursery that appeals to you, and make it a point to become a regular customer there. Go out of your way to be friendly, figure out which of the employees is best about answering your questions, and cultivate that relationship as carefully as you cultivate your garden. Having once established yourself there, you may still want to play the field for items your nursery doesn't have. Most nurseries don't carry many herbs, so you may have to go to an herb farm for them. And if you begin to favor certain varieties of seeds, you may have to order them from catalogues, since the catalogues offer many seeds not available in stores. But there is a wealth of information to be gained from nursery people, and that information is the least expensive item in their stock.

Now, about what to buy: It is a good idea to order a couple of seed catalogues around Christmas (addresses for these are listed in the back of this book), so that you can see what you have to choose from. (Seed catalogues are generally issued in January.) If you decide to order seeds from the catalogue, it's wise to place your order in January or February, before the spring rush begins.

Assuming that one of your reasons for gardening is to save money on your food bill, it's best to grow most of your vegetables from seed. But a few purchased seedlings may still be a necessity if you don't have a place to start seeds, or if you are just basically impatient. Tomatoes and green peppers, for example, won't always have time to mature if you plant the seeds directly in the garden after the danger of frost is passed, and so you must either start your seeds early in a protected, warm place, or buy plants. And in the case of herbs like marjoram or rosemary, one plant will be all you need, and the price of the plant may be no more than the price of a package of seeds. But for the vast majority of vegetables, started plants are an unnecessary luxury item. Some of the headstart you think you're getting with seedlings may be lost anyway since it will take them several days to recover from being transplanted.

Most started vegetable plants are sold in six-packs; that is, six little plants in one pot. Don't be greedy and choose the largest ones you can find; the larger the plants, the more likely they are to be a mass of overcrowded roots that will suffer greatly when you try to pull them apart. Choose plants that are small and vigorous, and you can minimize the transplanting trauma.

Other things you will have to spend money on in your first year of gardening include stakes for your peas, beans, and tomatoes, twine for the peas and beans to climb, and perhaps root stock for horseradish, asparagus, or berries. I have no desire to drive all the nurseries out of business; in fact, nothing gives me more pleasure than browsing through the nursery with a couple of dollars burning a hole in my pocket. But a part of the pleasure of gardening is the sense of self-sufficiency (however illusory) that comes from doing things yourself, and for that reason, if not out of economic necessity, some thought ought to be devoted to improvising your own equipment instead of buying it. If you have a stand of young alder, you can cut your own pea stakes. If you have friends who garden, you can trade seedlings and cuttings with them.

Tomatoes can be tied to their stakes with old nylon stockings or strips of cotton; old broom handles make good stakes.

A general rule of good gardening is to minimize your investment of money and maximize your investment of time. The goal of gardening is, after all, not to consume products, but to create produce.

Climate

No other area in North America enjoys the peculiar climate of our rainy region. Our climate is similar to that of southern England and part of Japan, and it is to the Japanese current that sweeps up the Pacific Ocean that we owe our mild winters, our bountiful rainfall, and our pleasant, gentle summers.

Extending from British Columbia south to the California border, and from the Pacific Coast east to the Cascade Mountains, the Pacific Northwest climate provides approximately 200 frost-free days per year, an abundant, though variable, rainfall, and a generally high level of humidity on which many vegetables thrive. There are, of course, variations within this general climate; as one climbs in elevation in the Coastal Range, for instance, the number of frost-free days will be fewer; and just east of the Olympic Mountains is a rain shadow in which the annual rainfall is considerably lower. Still, anyone who has lived here will agree on the hallmark of our common climate: it rains a lot.

The consequences of this climate for the vegetable gardener are much happier than those for the devoted sunbather. We get about 60 percent of the possible sunshine during the summer, which is generally enough to ripen tomatoes and corn nicely, yet little enough to satisfy the requirements of many of the cool-weather vegetables, such as cabbage, lettuce, and various other kinds of greens. We can't grow big watermelons or peanuts, it's true, and there's a good reason the cotton gin wasn't invented in the Pacific Northwest, but we can mourn these shortcomings over a bountiful feast of artichokes, peas, beans, squash, broccoli, peppers, eggplants, corn, and potatoes.

An understanding of our climate and a constant eye on the weather are prerequisites for good gardens, since the nature of the climate will affect where we locate our gardens, when we plant, and what sorts of vegetables we grow most successfully.

Site Selection. Our limited supply of sunlight is the first consideration in choosing a spot for our gardens. For all but the most adamant cool-weather crops, the sunniest location you can provide is best for your vegetables. For sunlovers like tomatoes, corn, peppers, and eggplant, a full day of sun (eight hours or more) is crucial. For maximum sunlight, an unobstructed southern exposure is best; an eastern exposure that gets plenty of morning sun is next best. The effectiveness of sunlight can also be increased by locating heat-loving vegetables on the south side of a white building that will reflect even more light and heat onto them.

Cool-weather vegetables tolerate more shade, and may, during a hot summer, even prefer it. If your sunny area is limited, you may want to maintain vegetables in two or more locations: the sun-lovers in the sunny place, and the rest in another, or scattered among flower beds and between shrubs.

Planting Times. Our climate also determines the best time to plant. Our last frosts in the spring are usually somewhere between the first of April and the middle of May. Many of the

vegetables we grow can withstand a little frost and can therefore be planted earlier. For the frost-hardy vegetables—
spinach, cabbage, carrots, and onions are some—planting
time is determined by the condition of the soil: if it's still too
wet and soggy from winter rains, seeds will rot instead of
sprouting. So for all those seed packages that direct us to
"plant as early as ground can be worked," we will decide on
the basis of how muddy our knees will get in the planting of
them, rather than how soon the ground thaws from winter
freezing.

This generally means that we start our gardens sometime
in late February or early March, with the planting of peas, and
that we continue the spring planting season through the
middle of May. And as some of these early crops mature and
are harvested we can continue to plant frost-hardy vegetables
that will mature in the fall from seeds sown in June and July.

For the frost-tender vegetables—corn, tomatoes, squash,
peppers, beans, and eggplant—planting must wait until May.
To determine when the danger of frost is passed, watch the
weather reports, and wait until the night-time temperatures
have stayed above freezing for a couple of weeks. The exact
time of planting will vary from year to year, and sometimes
even the most experienced gardeners will be foiled by an
unexpected cold spell late in the spring. When this happens,
tender plants must be covered at night with some improvised
covering, such as plastic bags held in place by stones, that
will protect them from damaging frost.

Selection of Vegetables. Our climate will also influence what
varieties of certain vegetables do best here. For the most part,
it is safe to follow the advice given in seed catalogues about
this, or to consult the people at the nursery or garden store
where you buy your seeds. I would hesitate to recommend

specific varieties of most vegetables because the seed companies are constantly hybridizing and changing them, and because new varieties of almost everything are constantly coming on the market.

But there are a few guidelines to follow in the selection of certain seeds and plants: The earliest varieties of vegetables that need a long, hot growing season, like tomatoes, peppers, eggplant, and corn should be chosen unless you have good reason to expect a long, hot summer. Most seed packages carry a listing of expected number of days from planting to harvest, and although that figure is based on ideal soil and weather conditions, it will at least give some basis of comparison between one variety and the next.

In the case of peas, there are a number of dwarf peas with vines that grow only three or four feet tall that are marketed in this area, even though they were developed for hotter climates where people need peas that will mature before the weather gets too hot. These dwarf peas may still be of some use to Northwest gardeners who, for whatever reasons, like short pea vines. Our climate, however, actually favors the use of the taller varieties, which are much more prolific and take up no more space.

There are also certain vegetables and fruits that won't do well at all during a cooler and rainier than average summer. There are years when eggplants just won't get enough heat to mature, and when we'll all have mountains of green tomatoes that will have to be brought indoors to ripen. Cantaloupe may produce abundantly during a hot summer, or not at all during a cool one.

This variability can be the cause of constant complaint. But whatever the weather is doing, it's good for something. If it's rainy and cool, you can be assured that your lettuce and broccoli are enjoying themselves, and if it's sunny and hot, your tomatoes and corn will be happy. And most years there will be a sufficient balance to bring you good harvests of everything.

Soils and Soil Preparation

Soil management is the most complex learning task of the vegetable gardener. A thorough understanding of soil formation and chemistry is not necessary for a good garden, and, in fact, would require several years of study. But the ability to recognize different soil types, a basic understanding of plant nutrition, and a working knowledge of fertilizers, soil additives, and the private lives of soil micro-organisms *is* necessary and should not be neglected.

DIFFERENT KINDS OF SOIL

Soil is created by geologic forces in a number of ways. Glaciers moving like giant bulldozers carried and deposited broken rocks and debris that became soil; wind and water weathered parent rocks into smaller particles; rivers carried silt down mountainsides and left it in the valleys; and a host of living organisms, fallen leaves, and dying trees contributed to the soil-forming process. These different geologic processes, over the past few million years, have created three distinct soil types in the region, each of them easily recognizable.

Sand. Sand, or sandy soil, is composed mostly of silicates. Pure sand is troublesome for the gardener because it contains

virtually no organic matter or plant nutrients, and doesn't hold enough water to keep plants from drying out.

Clay. Clay, or clay soils, have the opposite problem. Clay is composed of much smaller particles than sand, and these particles cling together to form hard clumps that are difficult for plants roots to penetrate. Clay soils are often so dense that water and air can't penetrate them, and are so slow to warm up in the spring that planting must often be delayed. Clay soils are generally richer in plant nutrients than sandy soils, but the nutrients in clay are usually not available to plants because of the texture of the soil, and because of its acidity.

Silt. Silt is that wondrous black stuff that is deposited by rivers in the valleys of the Pacific Northwest, often several feet deep, and rich in organic material. The fertility of silt may be affected by its source; that is, silt washed down from a bare mountain top would not be as fertile as that from lower elevations where there is abundant vegetation.

Most of the silt soils in the Northwest are commercially farmed, and for good reason. Silt is clearly the best of the Northwest soils. But lacking it, as most of us do, is no disaster. Taking a lesson from the geologic forces that created it, we can change the character of both sandy and clay soils to equal or better the growing qualities of silt.

The Best Soil for Vegetables

The soil requirements of vegetables are different than the requirements of our native vegetation in a number of ways.

The first of these differences is vegetables' preference for a soil that is only slightly acid. Our soils, because of our heavy rainfall and the nature of the vegetation that decomposes here, are quite acid. The Ph scale, with which every gardener should become familiar, measures the degree of acidity or alkalinity of the soil. On this scale, a measurement of seven denotes neutral; readings of less than seven measure the degree of acidity, and readings above seven the degree of alkalinity. Older gardeners, lacking this scientific scale, referred to acid soils as "sour," and to the process of correcting acidity as "sweetening" the soil.

Second, vegetables require near-perfect drainage; that is, the soil must retain enough water to keep the plants supplied with moisture, but must not be soggy, and must be porous enough so that water and air can move freely through it.

Growing vegetables also need a variety of nutrients, just as humans do. But while the goal of human nutrition is simply to stay alive and healthy, the goals of plant nutrition are more complex. Most vegetables not only need to stay alive and healthy, but also need to grow *fast*. Celery and radishes, for instance, will be stringy and bitter if they grow too slowly. Furthermore, by varying the amounts of different plant nutrients, it is possible to control what part of the plant will grow most vigorously. What you want from your tomato plants is tomatoes; what you want from lettuce is leaves. By supplying them with different nutrients, you can encourage fruit production in one plant, and green, leafy growth in another.

The three basic and essential plant nutrients are nitrogen, phosphorus (phosphates), and potassium (potash). Nitrogen is essential to green leafy growth, phosphorus is what makes plants bloom and bear fruit, and potash is important for strong healthy roots, and for general resistance to disease.

If you are unfamiliar with these three nutrients, you should take the time right now to memorize their names and functions. The following is a useful over-simplification: "Nitrogen/leafy growth; phosphorus/fruit; potassium/roots." It is an over-simplification because all three nutrients need each other to work effectively; that is, nitrogen alone will not produce a healthy green plant if there is no potassium present to nourish its roots, and phosphorus will not make tomatoes bear fruit if they are lacking in nitrogen to feed their leaves.

But by varying the proportions of these three nutrients, you can manipulate the plant's growth to suit your own needs.

It is this phenomenon that accounts for the production of some fertilizers that promise to make plants bloom and other that promise to make plants grow. The "blooming" fertilizer contains more phosphorus; the "growing" fertilizer more nitrogen. A more careful look at fertilizer labels will tell you what percentage of each of the three basic nutrients the fertilizer contains. On all fertilizer containers, there are three numbers, which list the percentages of nitrogen, phosphorus, and potash, in that order.

Fertilizers sold for vegetable gardens are usually labeled 5-10-10, that is, 5 percent nitrogen, 10 percent phosphorus, and 10 percent potash. The higher percentage of phosphorus is included to insure the success of heavy-fruiting crops like tomatoes and squashes, and the abundance of potash to insure the success of root crops like beets and carrots. But green leafy crops don't really need so much phosphorus and potash, and could just as well be given a 5-1-1 fertilizer.

There are, of course, organic or non-synthetic sources of all these nutrients as well. Animal manures are a good source of nitrogen, and generally contain small quantities of phosphorus and potassium. Blood meal and cottonseed meal are also good sources of nitrogen, as is liquid fish fertilizer. Bone meal is the best organic source of phosphorus, and wood ashes are the best source of potassium.

There are other "trace" elements necessary for good healthy plants; iron, sulphur, boron, copper, zinc, and manganese need to be present in the soil in small quantities. These trace elements can be supplied by commercial fertilizer, or by adding compost or manure to the soil.

Finally, a healthy soil for growing vegetables must contain a greater quantity of organic matter than nature has provided, unless you are among the fortunate few who live in a river valley full of silt. Organic matter is everything that was once alive that has decomposed and become part of the soil. You can observe the accumulation of organic matter on the floor of any forest, where falling leaves, dead trees, cones, branches, wildflowers, and other vegetation is constantly falling and decomposing, thus returning nutrients to the soil in

[21]

an endless cycle. This layer of thoroughly rotted organic matter is called humus.

All this vegetation doesn't decompose and turn into humus of its own accord; that feat is accomplished by millions of soil micro-organisms, and by worms and slugs that eat and digest vegetable matter and deposit rich castings in the soil. A healthy soil literally teems with bacteria and fungi, all busily working at converting dead or dying organic matter into usable plant food.

So the optimum soil for vegetables should be rich in organic matter, supply plenty of nitrogen, phosphorus, potassium, and trace elements. It should be only slightly acid and should be porous enough for air and water to move freely through it.

If you have survived this lesson in basic soil chemistry, you are ready to start planning your own program of soil management. The basic goal of your program will be to create a paradise for your vegetables. These are the objectives that must be achieved in order to create that paradise:

1. Supply humus, both as a source of nutrients, and to improve the "tilth" of your soil. Tilth refers to the texture of the soil; good tilth means that it is loose enough not to form hard clumps, that water and air are able to circulate properly through it, and, not the least important, that it is easy to work in.

2. Provide specific nutrients for plant growth; that is, nitrogen, phosphorus, potassium, and the necessary trace elements.

3. Correct acidity, so that your soil's Ph reading is between 6.0 and 7.0, except where acid-loving plants will grow. (Acid-loving plants are potatoes, strawberries, and blueberries.)

It should be understood that improvement of the soil is a continuing process that never really reaches a finished state. In the forest everything that grows eventually dies and is returned to the soil. In the vegetable garden a goodly proportion of what grows is taken away from the soil and eaten. Because of this interruption of the natural humus-producing cycle, as well as because of vegetables' need for greater quantities of humus, the vegetable gardener must continually add organic matter to the soil. Animal manures, compost, and green manure crops are used for this purpose.

SOURCES OF HUMUS

Animal manures are a wonderful source not only of humus but also of nitrogen and of smaller quantities of phosphorus, potassium, and some of the trace elements. Before the invention of chemical fertilizers, manure was highly treasured as a fertilizer—so much so that in some societies, a family's prosperity was judged by the size of their manure pile.

Today, it is harder, especially for the city-dweller, to find a source of good manure than it was a hundred years ago. Manure is sold in bags at nurseries and garden stores, but it is generally rather expensive. Some very large nurseries will sell manure by the cubic yard, which is somewhat more economical. If you are fortunate enough to have your own horses, cattle, chickens, or even rabbits, or if you have friends who have animals and are willing to share the bounty, this expense may not be a problem for you. If you will be buying manure, however, there are some questions you should ask about what you're getting before you make the investment.

The fertility of manure varies greatly according to how it has been handled, its age, and what it is mixed with. Most commercially available manure is the product of stable cleaning, and will include a fairly large percentage of animal bedding, that is, straw, sawdust, or woodchips. It is wise to ask what percentage of what you are getting is actually manure, and what percentage is bedding. The kind of bedding mixed with the manure will affect its usefulness in the garden, too. Manure that is mixed with sawdust or woodchips is of less value than that mixed with straw. Woodchips don't contain enough nitrogen to rot by themselves very well, so they "borrow" nitrogen from the soil for this purpose, thus causing a temporary depletion of the nitrogen supply in the soil. Thus, the nitrogen that would have been supplied by the manure is consumed by the rotting wood chips, rather than being available to nourish plants. The nitrogen content of the manure will be higher if the manure was taken from the stable or chicken coop, piled up, and covered rather than left lying out in the weather where rain can wash away valuable nutrients.

Various kinds of manure may vary considerably in the quantities of plant nutrients each contains. Chicken and rabbit manure are highest in nitrogen, followed by steer and horse manure. However, the greater mass of horse and steer manure provides more humus for the soil than the compact, concentrated manures of smaller animals. And, in my opinion at least, horse and steer manures are much more pleasant to handle than the small-animal manures.

The best animal manure is obtained by going through a pasture where horses or cattle are kept, shoveling it all into a wheelbarrow, and dumping it all into a large pile that is kept covered. This should be done once a week, so that the manure is not left lying in the pasture too long. Manure can also be added to the compost heap in alternating layers with garden and household wastes.

No animal manure should ever be added to the garden

until it has been allowed to rot for a few weeks. Applications of fresh manure may "burn" plants (a chemical burn caused by excessive amounts of certain forms of nitrogen). The full benefits of the nutrients in the manure won't be available for plant use until it has decomposed anyway.

How much manure you will need is a question to which there is no precise answer. I have never known anyone to have too much, however, and would say generally that you should make it your business to acquire as much manure as you can beg, borrow, shovel, or buy.

Compost is homemade humus, and contains all manner of plant nutrients, as well as a good supply of the soil microorganisms that are so essential in converting plant nutrients to forms plants can use.

There are countless ways to make compost, some of them not yet discovered. If you once understand the principles involved, you can invent your own method, or choose from one of the methods discussed later in this chapter.

The basic principle of composting is this: If you pile up a heap of vegetable matter, keep it damp, and cover it, it will rot and turn into humus. The quality of humus you get will vary with the sorts of vegetable matter you put in your pile. Generally the best humus comes from a compost pile that is composed of alternating layers of different kinds of matter—for example, a layer of kitchen waste followed by a layer of grass clippings followed by a layer of manure, etc.

Candidates for composting include weeds pulled from the garden; all unused portions of vegetable plants, such as pea vines, squash plants, corn stalks, etc.; grass clippings; leaves; manure; seaweed; and all food garbage from the kitchen, except grease and meat scraps.

In order for a compost heap to "finish," or complete the

process of becoming humus, you will have to quit adding to it and start a second heap. If the composting action of your heap is slow, you may end up with three heaps in different stages of decay, and you will have to rotate using them accordingly. When you start a new heap, you should turn the contents of the previous one (or two) over, so that the contents are mixed and air is incorporated into it to speed the rotting process.

A working compost heap will generate a fair amount of heat as it rots, and this heat is usually enough to kill weed seeds and insect eggs. It will not be hot enough to kill disease organisms, however, so no diseased plants should be composted.

Different methods of composting have been developed to accommodate different sizes of composting operations.

For apartment dwellers, or for those with small yards, vegetable matter can be composted in large plastic garbage bags, which can be hidden behind bushes or kept in the basement. They should be kept tightly closed, of course, and checked periodically to see that they are moist. For this and other methods of composting small amounts of vegetation, it's best to chop things up fairly small so that they'll rot faster.

For larger operations, large wooden boxes can be built to contain the compost. The best arrangement is a series of three large boxes, built side by side, and with a common lid that doubles as a place to chop up large items, such as corn stalks. As the first box is filled, its contents are turned and the second is started. By the time the third box is filled, the compost in the first box will be ready for the garden, and the cycle can start again.

The sides of the boxes need not be solid; wire or slatted sides will do so long as they are sturdy, and so long as the top is covered to prevent rain from washing through the compost pile and draining it of nutrients. This same method can be expanded for larger gardens simply by enlarging the size of the boxes.

For large places where the compost heap will be out of sight, it is possible simply to make a pile on the ground and cover it with a plastic tarp held in place by stones. Or, a pit can be dug and used as a composting place. Vegetable matter is really not fussy about where it rots.

How long a compost heap will take to finish is a highly variable matter. Chopping things up before you compost them speeds the process up, as does vigilance about keeping it damp, and turning it over occasionally. Woody things like tree branches and berry vines should not be composted at all unless they've been thoroughly chopped or put through a shredder, because they take a year or more to rot.

The process of rotting requires nitrogen, just as the growing process does, so materials high in nitrogen, like manure and grass clippings, will speed up the composting action. A handful of high-nitrogen fertilizer will do the same thing. There are also products called compost starters at the nursery, some of which are essentially nitrogen, and some of which are spores of the soil bacteria that actually perform the rites of rotting. These products are unnecessary unless you're really in a hurry to have finished compost.

Green manure crops are not manure at all, but derive their name from the benefits they provide for the soil which are, logically enough, quite similar to the benefits of animal manures. A green manure crop is a planting of grass, alfalfa, or vetch that is allowed to grow to about a foot tall and is then ploughed into the ground. This adds a good deal of organic matter to the soil and increases the soil's nitrogen supply. Green manure crops even have some advantages over animal manures: they don't contain weed seed, as animal manure does unless it has been thoroughly composted, and they will help crowd out weeds in the garden. And a stand of winter rye is nicer to look at during the winter than an empty garden.

Green manure crops are usually planted in the fall and ploughed under the following spring. Legumes such as alfalfa and vetch are the best of the green manure crops, since they can fix nitrogen from the air and store it in their roots. But they don't generally grow well west of the Cascades, and so either a mixture of vetch and winter rye, or just winter rye by itself is generally used here. Winter rye is also the cheapest seed, at least at the present time.

When a green manure crop is ploughed under, the garden should be left idle for two weeks before planting begins. Ploughing in such a crop stirs the soil bacteria into action, and it should be given a chance to do its work—that is, decomposing the rye—and then to settle down a bit. If you plant while all the soil bacteria are at the peak of activity, they may get carried away and go to work on the plants you set out too.

CORRECTING ACIDITY BY ADDING LIME

The cure for acidity is the easiest part of soil preparation; you simply spread lime on the garden and dig it in along with whatever else you're using. How much lime you need depends on how acid the soil is. You can either guess at this, as I do, or you can buy a small soil-testing kit and measure the Ph of your soil. Once you have measured the Ph you can follow the directions on the bag of lime to determine how much to add.

Guessing at the Ph level of your soil isn't really so chancy as it sounds; you can tell approximately how acid the soil is by what was growing there before. If your garden is surrounded by cedar or fir trees, it's probably more acid than if a stand of grass or clover prevailed there. If rhododendrons do well in your soil, it is more acid than if peonies thrive there. If your soil is quite acid, add one handful of lime for every two feet of row, or spread a 40-pound bag of lime over each 500 square feet. Do not, however, lime the places where you intend to grow potatoes, strawberries, or blueberries. Lime should be added each year since the natural tendency of the soil is to

[29]

return to its original level of acidity. However, the effect of digging humus into the soil year after year will help stabilize the Ph level, so that less lime will be needed with each passing year.

SOURCES OF SPECIFIC NUTRIENTS

In a garden to which organic matter and manure have been added for many years, little if any commercial fertilizer will be necessary. But for the first two or three years, before the soil has been significantly improved by these methods, the use of some fertilizer at planting time is worth the expense. If you prefer not to use chemical fertilizers, you can mix your own organic fertilizer with products from the nursery. Combine two parts blood meal or cottonseed meal (a source of nitrogen), one part bone meal (a source of phosphorus), and one part wood ashes (a source of potassium). The only disadvantage of the organic mixture is that it doesn't contain the trace elements found in commercially prepared fertilizer. However, the trace elements can be supplied by using manure or seaweed.

If you do use commercial fertilizer, there are a couple of things to watch out for. It's important to choose a fertilizer that is made for this area, since some fertilizers formulated for use in other parts of the country are marketed here even though they are not suited to Northwest soils. The problem is that they contain sulphur to increase the acidity of the soil and that is exactly what we don't need. The nitrogen in chemical fertilizers may also burn plants if the fertilizers are used in over-large quantities, or if the fertilizer comes in direct contact with the foliage or roots of young plants.

It's also a good idea not to rely on chemical fertilizers any longer than is necessary simply because they do nothing for

the health of the soil, will give worms a fatal case of indiges-
tion, encourage laziness in plants, and are often made of the
very petrochemicals we are trying (aren't we?) to conserve.

In a garden to which lots of manure and compost have
been added, a good handful of bone meal should still be
worked into the soil for each of the heavy-fruiting plants, such
as tomatoes and squash. And extra wood ashes will benefit
rows of root vegetables.

Liquid fish fertilizer is useful as an extra source of nitrogen
for plants that are especially heavy feeders. And, for the same
purpose, manure tea can be made by soaking manure in a
bucket of water for several hours, then pouring the water on
hungry plants.

SPECIAL SOIL PROBLEMS

If, to begin with, your soil is so compacted you can't get a
shovel to penetrate it, or if it is so sandy it belongs on the
beach, you have a special problem. For new gardens where
the soil is truly awful it may be wise to dig in as much organic
matter as you can, grow a spring green manure crop, plough it
under in the fall, and repeat the process, planting a fall cover
crop that will be ploughed in the following spring. This means
that your garden won't be usable for a full year while this
soil-improvement scheme is in progress, but if the soil is really
poor, it may save you a great deal of frustration. During the year
that it takes for all this, you can still plant a few vegetables in
flower beds or in containers.

If your soil is otherwise troublesome or unproductive, and
you can't figure out why, you can have it tested through the
British Columbia Ministry of Agriculture or the County Extension Program in your county. (See the Appendix for the location
of the Extension Program or Ministry of Agriculture Office

nearest you.) For five dollars you can learn everything you need to know about your soil and receive advice on how to improve its fertility. You may want to take their advice with a grain of salt, since they are likely to recommend chemical remedies rather than organic ones, but you can be confident that at least their diagnosis will be correct.

Soil testing is best done in the fall, since it takes several weeks to get the test results back, and you may need some time to fix whatever is wrong with your soil before spring planting.

A Survey of Gardening Methods

Over the centuries, people throughout the world have developed different methods of gardening to suit their particular soil and climate conditions. In hilly, steep country, people learned to build terraces to keep the soil from washing downhill; in wet, cool places they learned to build raised beds so that the soil would drain better and warm up sooner in the spring. Where land was scarce, ways were found to increase the yields of small gardens.

Whether one or more of these methods will be useful to you will depend on the specific soil conditions you start with, the amount of labor you are willing to invest, and what sort of garden you find most pleasing to look at.

FRENCH INTENSIVE

This method was developed to increase the yields of small gardens, but it will work in any size plot. It requires a good deal of work with the shovel, and an ample supply of manure and compost.

It differs from other methods of gardening in the special soil preparation required, as follows: Starting at one end of the garden, dig a trench two shovelfuls deep. Load the dirt from this into a wheelbarrow, take it to the opposite end of the garden, and dump it. Then, using either a shovel or a pickaxe, break up the soil in the bottom of the trench, and fill it half full of manure and compost. Just next to this first trench, dig a second, using the soil from the second trench to finish filling the first. Again, break up the soil in the bottom of the trench, and fill it half full of manure and compost. Repeat this process until you come to the other end of the garden, using the soil from the first trench to fill the last.

This super-cultivation and enrichment of the soil will enable it to support more plant life, and so vegetables can be planted closer together. Generally, such gardens are planted in beds four feet wide rather than in single rows, thus minimizing the amount of space used for paths. Plants are spaced close enough so that their outer leaves touch one another at maturity, thus shading the ground and conserving soil moisture.

CHINESE RAISED-BED METHOD

This method was developed by Chinese farmers who worked with problems familiar to Northwest gardeners: soggy soil that didn't drain properly, limited land areas available for cultivation, and a relatively short growing season.

This method, too, begins with a special method of soil preparation. Rocks and debris are removed from the soil, and the rocks are used to pave paths in the garden. Beds are measured and marked to be four feet wide and as long as convenience or the size of the garden dictate. Manure and compost are dug into the beds in enough quantity to raise the beds eight inches above the level of the paths between them. Then the raised beds are raked smooth on top, and a small trench is provided around the perimeter of each bed to catch water, so that the water doesn't run in the paths.

Once these permanent beds are established, they are used year after year, with annual additions of compost and/or manure. Because the drainage in raised beds is superior, they will warm up sooner in the spring, so that planting can begin a little earlier.

Like the French Intensive method, the raised-bed method also saves space otherwise used for paths or spaces between rows, and allows more plants to be grown in the same area than with conventional methods.

The book *Better Vegetables the Chinese Way* by Peter Chann with Spencer Gill (Graphic Arts Center Publishing Co., Portland, 1977) gives the details of this method, and shows how beautiful such plantings can be.

THE STOUT METHOD

This method has other names; it is also called the perpetual mulch method, and is sometimes referred to as "trash gardening." But it was Ruth Stout, who wrote a book called *Gardening Without Work*, who made it famous.

This method involves scarcely any soil preparation. Rather, the entire garden area is covered with a heavy layer of mulch, usually straw or grass clippings, and is never ploughed or dug up at all. At planting time, the mulch is pulled back from the rows and the seeds planted. Then, as the plants grow, the mulch is snuggled back around them. As the mulch rots, more is added, so that there is always a heavy enough layer to keep weeds from sprouting and to keep the soil moisture from evaporating. The idea is that this eliminates two of the most physically demanding garden chores: ploughing and

[35]

weeding. It also duplicates nature's own program of soil enrichment: as the mulch rots, it continually adds humus and nutrients to the soil beneath it, gradually building up an ever-thicker layer of rich topsoil.

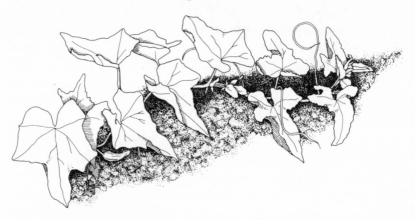

This method has distinct disadvantages for our climate, however. First of all, since our soils are more likely to be too wet than too dry, the heavy mulch may delay planting time in the spring by preventing the soil from drying out and warming up. Second, the mulch provides a haven for slugs and other insects, and for fungus diseases that develop in overly moist situations.

Also, it may be difficult and expensive to acquire the huge amount of straw or clippings that it takes to make this method work. To effectively prevent weed growth, a six-inch layer of straw is a minimum, and in any but the smallest gardens, that can end up costing a fair amount of money unless you have a free source of mulch.

There are effective uses for mulch: it is a good protective measure for plants that might otherwise freeze during the winter, and in an exceptionally dry year it might be a good idea for conserving water.

If mulches are used, it is necessary to give some thought to what materials will be used for the mulch. Wood chips or sawdust should be avoided, both because they take too long to rot, and because they may not contain enough nitrogen to rot by themselves, and will therefore "borrow" nitrogen from the soil for this purpose. This condition is known as "nitrogen deficit," since the woodchips are using nitrogen that ought to be available for plant growth, and will return it only after they've finished rotting. Straw and grass clippings, spoiled hay, or other leafy vegetable matter are the best sorts of mulch, since they rot more easily and are higher in nitrogen.

The best results from mulching are reported by gardeners who gather large quantities of seaweed and apply it, fresh from the water, to the entire garden. The wealth of minerals and plant nutrients in seaweed is reputed to produce marvelous tomatoes, and to improve soil fertility greatly. The odor of rotting seaweed may cause some temporary distress, but it disappears in a couple of weeks.

English Traditional

This is a pretty loosely defined method, and the one we are all most familiar with. Vegetables are planted in single-file rows, with enough room between each row to walk. (Whether or not the English invented it I don't know; I choose to call it English only because that's the gardening lineage I happen to come from.)

The advantages of this method are that it makes planning simple, requires no extraordinary preparation, and makes no extraordinary demands on the soil. Since rows are spaced far enough apart to walk between them, and since plants are not crowded into small spaces, each plant has a larger soil area to draw water and nutrients from without competition from its neighbors.

This method of laying out the garden can be varied by band planting; that is, planting rows twelve inches wide, so that smaller plants, such as carrots and green onions, are planted three or four across rather than in single file.

The disadvantages of this traditional method are that it may waste space, require more weeding and cultivation between all those rows, and may make your neighbors think you don't have much imagination.

NORTHWEST IDIOSYNCRATIC

This is no method at all, but it should be included nonetheless. The land itself in the Northwest is full of variety; in some places it is too wet, in others too dry, sometimes it needs to be raised in order to drain properly, and in other situations it may need to be mulched to keep from drying out too much. The Northwest gardener may, in a single garden, have an area of raised beds, an area that is planted in rows, an area that is mulched, and an area of particularly rich soil where the French Intensive method has been used. There may also be flower beds in the middle of the vegetable patch, or vegetables in the middle of the flower beds. Tomatoes may dangle from hanging pots by the front door, chives may bulge out of a pot on the window sill, and marigolds may interrupt a row of carrots. Gardening has always provided an opportunity for both creative thinking and idiosyncracy; the best Northwest gardeners use both to the fullest.

[38]

Good Garden Practices

The foundation of success in the garden is well-prepared soil in a fairly sunny location. To build on this foundation requires the development of gardening skills and a sensitivity to the needs of growing plants. This awareness of the working of plants doesn't mean that you have to talk to them; plants are poor conversationalists and I am not convinced that they even really listen to anything I tell them.

It is necessary, however, to spend a good deal of time look-ing at plants. This is no great hardship, and, to the uninitiated, may even appear as idleness. A bench, a chair, or an apple crate placed in some strategic vantage point is a good place to sit and survey the garden, making mental notes of what is about big enough to need thinning, what rows will be due for harvest soon, and a myriad of other observations necessary for planning upcoming garden activities. There is another way of looking at plants too: on hands and knees, pull leaves back to see how they grow, look at their undersides to see if anything's chewing on them, observe how tomato plants form foliage branches and fruiting branches so you'll know which ones to prune. Both the overall view of the garden and its needs and the close-up inspection of individual plants are a

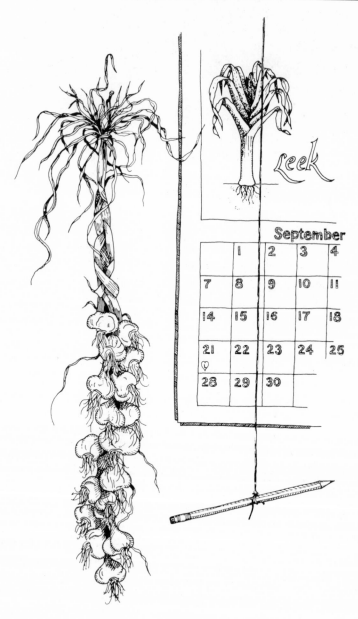

Leek

September

	1	2	3	4
7	8	9	10	11
14	15	16	17	18
21	22	23	24	25
28	29	30		

necessity to the immediate success of this year's garden and to the long-range development of your own gardening skills.

If you plan to grow much more than a potted tomato plant, it will probably be necessary to perform a couple of simple tasks with paper and pencil. First comes a list of what you want to grow, second a drawing of your garden space and what you will plant where. These are tasks to be done carefully and thoughtfully; plans must be drawn with consideration for plants' varying heights, and their differing needs for sunlight and moisture. If, when you plant, your plantings differ from what you've drawn, that should be recorded on paper too. Labeling rows with the seed packages is generally insufficient; the printing on many seed packets will fade away entirely in sunlight, and a few good rains will reduce them to shreds. It is a better practice to keep track of your garden on paper kept in the house, and to save the seed packages along with your plans, since you may want to consult the directions on the empty packages for thinning or other special care later.

After you have decided what you want to grow, and before you draw your plan, read the section in Part Two about each vegetable on your list. Knowing the different soil, sun, and moisture needs of different plants will help you decide what should go where in your garden. Squashes, for instance, like lots of moisture, so if there is a place in your garden that tends to be moist, that is the place for them.

The garden layout must also take into account which vegetables will grow so tall that they might rob sunlight from their neighbors. Corn, beans, and peas are generally planted at the north end of the garden for this reason, but a calculating

[41]

gardener may want to make use of that shade for heat-shy plants like lettuce or radishes.

Perfecting a garden plan may take several hours of thought and contemplation, but that is as good a way to spend a rainy evening in February as any, and with a fire in the hearth and a glass of good sherry, it can be downright pleasant.

Some gardeners also keep a journal of what is planted when, the date of its maturity, and the crop's yield. Data on the weather, observations about the relative value of different varieties of the same vegetable, brilliant insights, poems, and idle doodling can also be kept in the same book.

COMPANION PLANTING

In uncultivated land, many different kinds of plants grow together, sometimes because they all like the same sort of soil, but also usually because each variety of plant contributes something of value to its neighbors. Tall trees in the forest provide shade for ferns and salal; the ferns and salal, in turn, keep the soil from washing away from tree roots. These mutually beneficial groups are called "natural associations." The same principle, when applied by humans, is called "companion planting." Lettuce plants that don't like the hot afternoon sun can be planted where they'll be shaded by tomatoes or beans; onions, garlic, or mint can be planted with cabbage to confuse the noses of moths sniffing out cabbages to lay their eggs on. And dill planted with the tomatoes is said to repel the tomato worm.

Many of the traditional companion planting combinations may have no value other than as quaint traditions, but some of them have been tested by agricultural experts and found to be worth doing. Marigolds have proven effective in repelling root nematodes (tiny little worms that damage vegetable

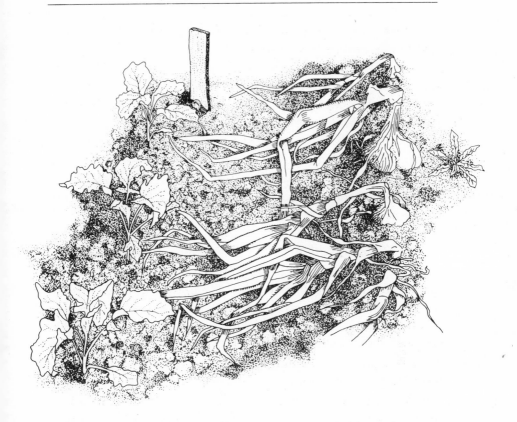

roots) because of an odor given off by marigold roots. The odor of fennel, on the other hand, repels most other plants, so fennel should be kept out of the garden. Insects generally don't like piquant vegetables such as onions and garlic, and so plantings of these interspersed throughout the garden will help to reduce the pest population.

Other companion plantings may have more directly physical advantages: beans are sometimes planted with corn, so that the beans will grow up the corn stalk and therefore eliminate the need for staking. Cucumbers will climb up

[43]

sunflowers, and big, vining squashes will grow over and hide ugly tree stumps.

PLANTING SEEDS

With the exception of tomatoes, eggplant, and peppers, which need to be given a headstart indoors in order to have time to mature after danger of frost is passed, seeds can be planted directly into the soil outdoors. If you are in a hurry for early crops, there may be some advantage in starting a few cabbages, lettuce plants, or broccoli indoors, but this is not a necessity.

The first seeds to be planted, around the first of March, will be peas, radishes, lettuce, and spinach. Sometimes seeds planted this early will get overly soggy and rot rather than sprout; or sometimes, because of relatively cold temperatures, they will take a very long time to germinate. Onion sets can be planted at this time too; they rarely fail to sprout, and seem to enjoy the blustery March weather. Cabbages, broccoli, and cauliflower can be sown around this time too, although, as with the other early plantings, there is some risk of poor or slow germination.

A second planting time comes around the first of April, when carrots, beets, parsnips, chard, and all the other frost-hardy vegetables can be sown. Seed potatoes can also be planted at this time. For many gardeners, this April planting time may also include the very early vegetables others plant in March; some people just don't like to gamble on planting any earlier than April.

Only when the danger of frost is passed, usually sometime in May, should the frost-tender vegetables be planted. Beans, cucumbers, squash, and corn can be sown directly in the garden, and started plants of tomatoes, peppers, and eggplant set out at this time.

Later in the summer successive crops can be sown as early crops are harvested and space becomes available. These later sowings should include crops that you will want to keep for winter use; carrots and other root vegetables planted in July can be left in the ground in the fall, and harvested as they are needed until December, or until the ground gets too soggy for them to keep well.

Large seeds, such as beans, peas, and corn, can be sprouted in the kitchen between wet paper towels before they are planted outside. If kept damp, they will begin to sprout in two or three days. This is not essential, but it hastens germination a little, and since any seeds that fail to sprout can be discarded before they are put in the garden, you can plant the sprouted seeds in exactly the spacing you want so that you won't have to thin them later.

STARTING SEEDS INDOORS

If you have a sunny windowsill or porch, you can save the expense of buying bedding plants by starting your own tomatoes, peppers, and other crops indoors. You will need containers for all the seedlings, but these needn't be purchased either; you can save milk cartons and cut off the tops and punch holes in the bottom for drainage, or use any other container that comes to mind. The specific advantage of milk carton bottoms is that when it's time to transplant the seedlings out into the garden, you can cut the corners of the milk carton down to the bottom and slide the plant, roots, soil and all, right into its spot outside without significantly disturbing it.

[45]

Good garden soil mixed with finished compost is the best medium for starting plants indoors, but it should be sterilized first as a precautionary measure against soilborne diseases that may cause seedlings to wilt. Soil can be sterilized by putting it in a large, shallow pan in the oven for 45 minutes at 200 degrees. Be sure to run your fingers through the soil and remove the worms before you do this.

In order to avoid transplanting seedlings from one pot to another, it's best to start with containers that are large enough to accommodate each plant until it is large enough, and the weather warm enough, for it to go outdoors. Half-gallon milk cartons are about the right size for tomatoes, peppers, and eggplant; quart milk cartons will suffice for lettuce, broccoli, cabbage, and most others. The containers that hold young plants should sit on a tray that will catch the drainage water from them; this tray can be a cookie sheet, or better yet, a kitty litter box with a couple of inches of clean litter in it. The kitty litter will absorb the excess water from the plants, and, as this water evaporates, it will create an island of humidity around the seedlings that protects them from the overly dry air found in most homes.

Two or three seeds should be planted in each container. The soil should be moistened before the seeds are planted, and the seeds covered with soil and pressed down lightly. Once the seedlings are up, all but the strongest plant in each container should be removed by snipping them off at ground level with scissors. The containers should be turned every day so that young plants don't fall over as they bend toward the light, and a careful watch should be kept to see that they are never allowed to dry out completely.

The problems most often encountered in starting seeds indoors are those of spindly, weak plants, usually caused by

[46]

lack of sufficient light, and a weak or leggy growth, caused by household temperatures that are too warm. Night temperatures for seedlings should be no more than 60°F (15°C); daytimes should not rise above 70°F (21°C). Even cooler temperatures are preferred by cool-weather vegetables, such as lettuce and cabbage. To increase the amount of light that young plants get, cover a large piece of cardboard with aluminum foil and prop it up behind them; this reflected light will nearly double the effectiveness of the available light and will obviate the necessity for turning the containers around every day.

Most plants should be started from six to eight weeks before they are to go outdoors; for tomatoes, eggplants, and peppers, eight weeks is the minimum.

Plants that are started indoors will need a period of a week or more to adjust to outdoor conditions before they are set out in the garden. This "hardening off" process begins with setting young plants outdoors for a few hours during the day, then leaving them out at night in a protected place for a couple of days so that they gradually become acclimated to the cooler outdoor temperatures. Only after this is done should they be carefully transplanted to the garden spot where they will mature.

If your house lacks a sunny windowsill, seedlings can be started indoors in the same manner with the aid of a growing light. And for cool-weather crops, you may want to build a cold frame, in which plants can be started outdoors and still be given some protection from inclement weather. The cold frame is a bottomless box about seven inches high filled about half full of good soil mixed with compost, and covered by salvaged windows or clear plastic. Cold frames can also be equipped with electrical heating cables under the soil to provide additional warmth, and the top can be raised and lowered to provide ventilation during the day and protection from cold at night. A thermometer stuck in the soil will aid in monitoring the temperature. Efficient use of a cold frame will require some experimentation and experience.

THINNING AND TRANSPLANTING

One of the most common faults of new gardeners is the failure to thin seedlings sufficiently. It is understandably difficult to pull up little plants that have so obligingly sprouted from seeds you planted with your own hand, but this apparent cruelty is one of those grim necessities of life that just have to be accepted. The consequence of not thinning properly is a poor harvest, for ten overcrowded plants will produce less food than three or four properly spaced ones every time.

There are two ways to do this thinning: one is to pull up and compost (or eat) excess seedlings; the other is to dig them up and move them from the seedbed to a more spacious location. In either case, this is work that must be done carefully, so that the roots of the seedlings are disturbed as little as possible. Thinning and transplanting must be done when plants are no more than three or four inches tall; if you wait longer, it will be next to impossible to move them without damaging their roots.

To thin plants in the row where the seeds were planted, the easiest method is to snip off the excess plants at the ground with a small pair of scissors. This will insure that, in the process of removing some plants, you don't disturb the roots of the plants that will remain. As you do this, put one finger on either side of the plant that will remain so that you don't accidentally cut it too. If you are thinning plants that are edible in their infancy, such as lettuce, you may want to thin twice. The first thinning, done when plants are about three inches tall, can leave twice as many plants as there will be room for;

[48]

the second thinning, done a couple of weeks later, should leave plants as much space as they will need to mature. This will give you two batches of thinnings for the table, and still leave your final crop with as much room as it needs to produce abundantly.

Where small plants are to be moved from a seedbed or from containers where they've been started indoors, even more care must be taken. Transplanting should never be done in a hurry, or on a day when you feel grouchy or impatient. Cool, cloudy days are best for this work, for if it is very sunny and warm, the roots of newly transplanted plants will almost certainly have trouble keeping up with the demands of the foilage for water, and the plants will wilt badly. (They may recover from this in a few days, but the extra stress will have slowed their growth; such stress may cause foilage plants, such as lettuce, to bolt and go to seed rather than produce more leaves.)

The ground where transplants are to be set should be prepared in advance, so that the young plants spend the least possible amount of time in transit. If you're working with plants that have been started indoors, it is then a simple enough matter to carefully remove them from their containers and set them in the ground. Both the plants you are moving and the ground you are moving them to should be thoroughly watered a few hours before the transplanting operation begins.

In the case of young plants that are to be moved from a cold frame or seedbed, even more care must be taken. Put a couple of inches of tepid water in the bottom of a bucket, and, with a trowel, carefully loosen the soil under the plants. Never try to pick the plants up by their foilage as this is certain to tear their roots. Pick them up from underneath the roots, along with the soil, and carefully separate any roots that are tangled together. Then put the roots of the seedlings in the water. When

[49]

you've got about a dozen plants separated and into the bucket, cover exposed roots in the seedbed, and go put the ones you've uprooted into the row where they will mature. Working in small batches this way will insure that no plants are out of the ground for more than a few minutes, and will help to minimize the trauma.

When setting the plants in the row, be sure that the roots are spread out below the plant as they were before you moved it. The most crucial task of these roots will be to re-establish their ability to draw moisture from the soil to keep the plants from wilting, and to do this, they must not be crowded together or left too close to the surface of the soil.

If, even after you've exercised the utmost care, your seedlings still wilt after they've been transplanted, don't give up hope. If you've been careful, they will probably recover within a few days. It is important that they be kept moist for a week or so after they've been moved; then the amount of water you give them should be gradually reduced. Some gardeners give transplants a light feeding of manure tea, fish fertilizer, or a special transplanting mix just after they've been moved. If your soil is in good condition, this probably isn't necessary, but certainly won't do any harm.

WATERING

The right amount of water at the right time is essential to all vegetables, for although they may survive dry spells, their flavor and quality will be impaired as a result. And, if plants are kept too wet, roots may rot or disease may set in.

For germinating seeds and for very young seedlings, daily watering (except during rainy spells, of course) will be necessary. This should be done with a fine, gentle spray from the hose, so that seeds and seedlings are not washed away by a blast of water.

Once plants are well established, however, watering habits must change. Most plants don't like to have their foliage sprayed with water. They react to such treatment about the same way you would if you were lying in the sun and someone squirted you with the hose. The water is needed by their roots, under the soil, and that is where the water must go. If your vegetables are planted in furrowed rows, this can be accomplished by filling the furrows with water. If your garden is arranged in raised beds, the water must be applied more slowly so that it has a chance to sink into the soil rather than run off the sides of the raised bed. For this a soaker hose (one with small holes all along it) can be laid between the plants, with the holes facing the ground.

How often you will need to water depends on your soil and how fast it drains. Check the soil for dryness by digging down four or five inches with a trowel. It doesn't matter if the soil is dry on top, but if it is dry five inches down, or close to it, water is needed.

This measurement applies to plants that are well established and have fairly deep roots, but there are a few crops that require moist soil closer to the surface. Lettuce and other green leafy crops should be kept fairly moist all the time.

Watering is best done in the early morning. When done at this time, a minimum of water will be lost to evaporation, and the plants will be getting the water when they need it—at the beginning of their day. The worst time to water is during the heat of the afternoon. As much as 50 percent of the water given at this time will be lost to evaporation, and the soaking with very cold water during the warmest part of the day is shocking to plants. If morning watering is impossible, late afternoon or early evening is next-best. If watering is done late in the day, however, care should be taken that plants are not left dripping wet as night falls, since various fungus diseases and blights are encouraged to grow by the combination of darkness and moisture, especially during the warmest part of the summer.

Over-watering is unnecessary, wasteful, and often harmful to growing plants. It should be scrupulously avoided.

An alternative to the usual garden hose is a system called drip irrigation, whereby specially laid pipes drip water constantly into the soil. This keeps the soil moisture at a constant level throughout the growing season and is said to save a great deal of water. For most home gardeners, the installation of such a system may be prohibitively expensive, but there is a "poor-gardener's" version of the same system that works nearly as well: Punch several holes in a three-pound coffee can and set it into the ground up to its brim near the plants to be watered. Fill it with water, and let the water drip through the holes in the can to keep the plants near it happy. This arrangement has the added advantage that you can fill the can with manure tea or liquid fertilizer from time to time and thus feed your plants as you water them.

Needless to say, the use of this method will require some experimentation to see how many holes should be punched in the can, and how large an area each can will keep supplied with water. This will depend on the draining qualities of your soil.

Some of the water in the can is bound to evaporate, creating a slightly more humid environment around it. This is a worthwhile advantage in watering artichokes, which enjoy a combination of warmth and humidity.

WEEDING

Most people think of weeding as the "housework" of gardening, a matter of cleanliness and appearance. There are other, more important reasons for pulling weeds, though: the weeds compete with your vegetables for space, soil nutrients, and light. Weeds may also provide shelter for slugs and insects.

The most efficient way to weed a garden is faithfully to pull out weeds by the roots while they are still small. If this is done several times during the early part of the growing season, none of the weeds will have a chance to go to seed or reproduce themselves, and so the weed population will gradually be mostly eliminated. A few weeds will continue to pop up later in the summer, but these will not be numerous.

Some gardeners consider weeding and cultivating part of the same operation. With a sharp hoe, they simultaneously break up the surface of the soil and chop up the weeds. This still leaves the weeds growing in among the plants to be pulled by hand, since using a hoe too close to the plants would damage their roots. Hoeing leaves the roots of the weeds still in contact with the soil, where they may recover and keep growing.

Piles of pulled weeds, thinnings, and other garden refuse should always be removed from the garden and put into the compost as soon as possible, for these piles attract insects and may be starting places for disease.

VOLUNTEERS

In the language of gardening, "volunteers" refers not to people who offer to help you in the vegetable patch, but to plants that appear where you didn't plant them. A single stalk of dill left to go to seed in the garden will result in little dill plants popping up everywhere the following spring, even though you've ploughed, raked, and otherwise rearranged the soil. Many other vegetables will do the same—potatoes are the most notorious, since you always miss a few of them when you dig them up in the fall, and those left in the ground will be sure to sprout the following spring.

Should you leave these volunteers there to grow or not? In most cases, it is best to pull them, since they will disrupt your garden plan and interfere with the growth of the crops you've planted. A volunteer tomato plant isn't likely to survive in the squash patch, and probably wouldn't produce much fruit anyway, since tomato volunteers don't usually germinate until late spring. Volunteer potatoes, unless the soil is piled up around them, will produce potatoes deep in the soil, where they'll be hard to get at in the fall. But volunteer dill is harmless enough if there isn't so much of it that it will shade out other crops, and if it won't be in your way. Volunteer lettuce plants can be dug up and put in the row with their fellows, or left to mature if they are in an advantageous spot.

With any other volunteers, it will be a matter of choice whether to let them grow or pull them, but if they are left to grow, they will naturally have to be watered and cared for just like the rest.

CROP ROTATION

If the same crop is grown in the same location year after year, the soil will soon suffer from depletion of the particular nutrients that that crop requires. The diseases and insects that thrive on that particular crop will then move in, and big trouble will follow. For these reasons, it is wise to re-arrange your planting every year so that different kinds of plants take turns in each part of the garden. Corn, a big plant that makes heavy demands on the soil, should be followed by peas or beans, which draw their nitrogen from the air, and leave some behind for the soil in their roots. Likewise, root crops should be followed by leafy ones, and heavy-fruiting vegetables such as squash should be followed by lighter, less demanding plants.

Generally speaking, the same plant should not be grown in the same spot more than once every third year. If you save your garden plans from year to year, you will have a record of what grew where to aid your crop-rotation planning.

If you have only one spot sunny enough to grow tomatoes, and therefore can't rotate this particular crop, extra care must be taken to replenish the specific nutrients this crop requires. Extra phosphorus should be added annually, and more generous supplies of compost and manure should be worked into the soil. Even so, bugs and diseases may become a problem, and you may have to resort to growing tomatoes in containers for a season or two to give the soil a change of plant life and a chance to recover its balance.

HARVESTING

Keeping a close watch on your garden will pay off when it comes time to harvest, for vegetables have a sneaky habit of all ripening at once if your back is turned. Most vegetables that you buy in the market are harvested when they are as big as they will get, but the peak of their flavor may actually come sooner, while they are younger and more tender. Peas, beans, summer squashes, and many other vegetables are tastier if they're picked slightly immature, but it would not be to a commercial farmer's advantage to pick them then, since he sells them by the pound, and this would reduce his yield. But

for the home gardener it is a good practice to start harvesting while vegetables are still young, since this extends the length of the harvest and encourages the plants to keep bearing.

Even in small gardens, there will be surpluses of some crops, that is to say, the time will come when you really don't want to eat green beans for the fourth night in a row. These surpluses can be canned, frozen, or dried, depending on your taste and your technology. This is one of those tasks, like milking cows, that demands to be done on nature's schedule rather than your own. Snow peas, for instance, will become tough and stringy if they aren't picked at the proper time, and they will lose their flavor if they are picked and left sitting around for very long. For canning and freezing, it's best to have everything ready in the kitchen before you go out and pick the vegetables, so that the period between picking and preserving is kept to a minimum.

The best time of day for harvesting most vegetables to be frozen or otherwise preserved is in the early morning when they are freshest and most crisp. As with watering, the second best time is in the evening, and the worst time is during the middle of the afternoon, when greens are likely to be a little wilty. For tomatoes, corn, peppers, and eggplant, any time of the day will do. For vegetables to be eaten fresh, there is no reason to pick them before the table is set for dinner.

Pests and Diseases

"Healthy plants in a healthy soil" is still the best preventive measure against insects and disease. Plants are more likely to be heavily damaged by insects and disease if they are lacking in nutrients, if their root systems are constricted by soil that is too heavy, or if they have too much or not enough water. The balance of nature is indeed a matter of balance: the right amount of all the necessities of life and health are always the best insurance that health and vigor will continue.

Large areas of the same kind of vegetable (known as monoculture) are more likely to attract insect or disease problems than mixed plantings (known as polyculture). Rotating crops, mixing plantings, and making use of companion planting combinations all help to prevent trouble.

If these practices are followed, chances are that you will not have serious insect problems. I have known gardeners who grew vegetables in the same plot for upwards of twenty years without encountering troubles, simply because they understood and practiced a constant program of soil enrichment, rotated their crops, used companion planting combinations, and watered properly at the right times. Such good fortune is common, but not universal.

If a close watch is kept on the garden, any trouble that does strike can be spotted early, while there is still time to make a thoughtful study of the alternatives available for dealing with it. A few aphids found lurking on the underside of a leaf are no cause for panic, but may be the occasion for some thought about why they are attacking this plant in this location in the garden. Is the plant in good health? Does it have enough water? Are there plants you might put nearby that would repel the aphids?

If an infestation is found when only a few plants are affected, it may be possible to remove the infested leaves and burn them to avoid more immediate trouble; then a repellent crop should be planted nearby to prevent a recurrence.

Diagnosis of trouble is not always as simple as finding the culprit in the act, however. There are two major classes of trouble: those above the ground, such as chewing, sucking, and boring insects, and those in the soil itself, which include the larval stages of certain insects, soil-borne diseases, and certain kinds of molds and blights. The first task in diagnosing a plant that doesn't look well is to determine whether the trouble is coming from above the ground or below it. If you can't find evidence of direct damage to leaves, or any sign of insects, dig up the afflicted plant and examine its root system. This procedure is almost certain to produce a correct diagnosis, but if the worm or insect you find is unfamiliar to you, knowing the cause of the trouble may not be enough. If that is the case, put the plant and the insect or worm in a plastic bag and take it to your nursery for more information. And if that doesn't help, consult the list in the Appendix for the Government agency in your area, then call them for information about how to make use of their plant pathology services. In both the case of nurserymen and extension agents, you can be pretty sure that their identification of the trouble will be correct, but you may want to eschew their advice, since it will probably involve the purchase of pesticides you'd rather keep out of your food. If pressed, both nurserymen and extension agents can usually tell you about an organic remedy for your particular problem, but, of course, no one profits from home remedies but the person who uses them. If your nurseryman is so kind as to offer this sort of advice, the least you can do is to buy a package of seeds or a ball of twine while you're there.

It is also often the case that a plant will look poorly for more than one reason. If the soil is lacking in a particular nutrient, the trouble may be a combination of nutritional deficiency and consequent insect infestation, and/or disease. If this is the case, the diagnosis and cure may require considerable detective work to determine the needs of the soil, the cure for disease, and perhaps a repellent for the insects.

It would be impossible to list in a book such as this, all the insect and disease troubles that can afflict a garden, and even more impossible for the reader to make use of the information, since the more precisely one attempts to describe an insect or disease, the more technical and confusing the descriptions become. Furthermore, since I plant my carrots in a different place each year, I have never seen a carrot rust fly, and honestly couldn't tell you what one looks like, though I am told they are fairly common. (In this case, ignorance is bliss.)

Here is what I know about the most common Northwest pests:

Slugs, which are almost universal in Northwest gardens, can be controlled by talking a walk in the garden at dusk every evening with a salt shaker in hand. Sprinkle salt on them and they die. Better yet, put a little salt in the bottom of an empty can or carton, and, with a gloved hand, pick up the slugs and

BRUSSELS SPROUTS
LONG ISLAND IMPROVED
39¢

pop them in. This will prevent the buildup of excess salt in your soil. Look under leaves and in nooks and crannies to find their hiding places. If that seems too time-consuming, bury a pie plate up to its rim and fill it with beer. The slugs are attracted to the beer, and will fall in and drown in it. If the sight of a pan full of stale beer and dead slugs offends your delicate sensibilities, a jar made of opaque glass will do as well. Then when the time comes to remove it, you can slap on the lid without looking inside and toss it in the garbage can. (The waste of a recyclable jar will then be on your conscience.) If the slugs really get out of hand, you may want to resort to slug bait, but this is a powerful poison that will kill anything that eats it, including birds, small wild animals, and household pets. If you must, use slug bait in a slug trap which makes the bait available to slugs but not to birds or other animals. (Slug traps are advertised in some seed catalogues, and are also available from Walt Nicke, 19 S. Columbia Turnpike, Hudson, New York 12534. They cost $4.50 for ten traps, plus a 50¢ shipping charge.) Or, you can devise your own slug trap: bury a pie plate up to its rim, put in a little bait, then make a dome of chicken wire large enough to cover the pan, and bury the bottom three inches of the chicken wire in the soil around it. The slugs will crawl through the chicken wire to their death, but birds and other small animals won't be able to get to the bait. Even with these measures, it will be necessary to pick up and remove the dead slugs, since birds who may eat them will ingest the poison that killed the slug.

Next to slugs, probably the most common pest is aphids, which come in a wide range of colors, the most familiar of which is a pale green. Aphids are most likely to appear in hot weather, when they will gather in small hordes, usually on the undersides of leaves on the plants they choose to infest. If you watch your garden closely, it's pretty easy to find aphids before they spread and to remove and burn the affected leaves or plants. A cold spray from the hose that washes them off the plants may also be sufficient; if they are very young, they may not be able to get back to the plants before they expire. Giving the plants a bath with soap and water is also effective. Mint, garlic, and other smelly plants repel aphids. Ladybugs will also control aphids and are available through most seed catalogues. If you decide to use ladybugs in your garden, be careful that you don't release so many of them that there aren't enough bugs to keep them in business; if you do, they will all leave. Extra ladybugs can be stored in a jar in the refrigerator for several weeks, where they will remain in a state similar to suspended animation. In addition, if you use ladybugs, you must commit yourself to not using *any* pesticides of any sort, or you will be working at cross-purposes.

Flea beetles are distinctive little black bugs that chew neat round holes in the leaves of potatoes, peppers, tomatoes, and some other plants and jump like fleas when they are disturbed. You have to look closely to see them, but the tiny holes in the leaves of your plants will give away their presence. If flea beetles are found on potatoes, immediate action should be taken to get rid of them, for they will reproduce, and their offspring will burrow into the soil and damage potatoes. Pulling up the potatoes won't help; though potatoes are usually the first to be affected by flea beetles, they will eat other crops, and they move too fast to be treated like aphids. Rotenone is an effective and fairly safe pesticide that can be sprinkled lightly on affected plants. Rotenone is the ground-up root of the derris plant, and although it is toxic to insects and fish, it will not harm warm-blooded animals. It is also non-persistent; that is, it loses its effectiveness after ten days, and won't build up in the soil. The single caution about using rotenone is that it is toxic to bees, and so it should not be used when plants are blooming. Rotenone will also be washed away by rain, and so more than one application may be needed.

Blights and fungus diseases are largely preventable by proper watering and by making sure that plants are not left wet at night. Still, a warm rain in August or September may bring them on. Leaves and fruit will develop black, rotten looking spots and, if the disease is virulent, whole tomato vines may turn black and wither. This, too can usually be prevented by spotting the trouble early and removing the affected plant parts. If it does get out of hand, there is no recourse but to pull up the plants and salvage what you can. Commercial farmers may use fumigants and fungicides because for them the failure of a crop may mean bankruptcy, but the chemicals used to wipe out fungus diseases make no distinctions between the disease organism and the other beneficial life forms in the soil, and so wipe them all out. The effect is sterile soil that must then be artificially enriched with chemical fertilizers in order to produce crops, and the spiral of increasing needs for more and more chemicals becomes inevitable.

The sort of blight I have described is generally not persistent; that is, it will be safe to plant crops on soil where late-summer blights have occurred the previous year without fear of their recurrence. There are other soil-borne diseases, however, that are more troublesome and harder to get rid of. Club root, a soil-borne disease that deforms the roots of cabbage family plants and other greens, is an example. It must be starved out by the absence for four or five years of the crops it affects. Soil infected with this disease can be used to grow plants that are not affected by it, such as corn, tomatoes, peppers—anything but cabbage family plants, lettuce, and other greens.

Soil-borne maggots and worms that eat plant roots are easier to deal with. The carrot rust fly lays its eggs on the carrots' foliage, and the larvae burrow into the soil and eat the carrots. A similar type of fly larvae eat the roots of cabbage, sometimes causing a plant that looks healthy one day to topple over the next. These sorts of pests are preventable by disguising the smell of the plants needing protection, either by companion plantings of onions, mints, or fragrant herbs, or by using a spray made of water that onions and/or garlic have been boiled in. Incorporating generous amounts of wood ashes into the soil for root crops and cabbage-family crops is a good deterrent; a mound of wood ashes around the base of cabbage plants is also a good preventive measure. If you don't take preventive measures, and come out one morning to find one or more of your cabbage plants looking sickly, you will have to carefully dig them up, find and remove the maggot, and then replant them after mixing a generous supply of woodashes in the soil around their roots.

Diazinon is also used for killing off these soil-borne pests, and is generally regarded as a safe pesticide since it decomposes after about ten days. But the preventive measures work just as well and spare the lives of your friends, the earthworms.

New pesticides are always coming on the market, and many may tempt you with their claims of instant salvation from a host of real or imagined threats to your garden. But there is no such thing as a free lunch, and every benefit from a chemical has its corollary hazard. And, though public pressure on governmental agencies may have some effect on more careful testing of chemicals before they are released for public use, it is more often the case that the newer a pesticide is, the less it has been tested for possible ill effects on the environment.

Part Two

Growing...

ANISE: Anise is an annual herb with a mild licorice flavor and several uses. Its leaves can be chopped in salads or soups, and its seeds can be used in breads, applesauce, and confections.

Anise is easily grown from seed in any place that gets at least four hours of sun a day. Fertilizer and care are wasted on anise; it actually seems to prefer neglect. (The most luxuriant growth of anise I've ever seen was in a vacant lot in downtown Seattle.) Anise looks very much like dill, but would make pickles taste terrible, so be careful to label your plantings if your sense of smell is weak.

You can begin cutting leaves for salads or soup as soon as the plants are well established. In the late summer, when seeds have formed, cut the plants at the ground and store them, upside down, in a large paper bag in a warm, dry place. When they have dried, the seeds will fall to the bottom of the bag, where they can be collected and then stored in tightly closed jars for winter use.

ARTICHOKES: Artichoke plants can be started from seed either indoors or in the garden when the ground is warm, but since one or two plants will be enough for most families, it may be no

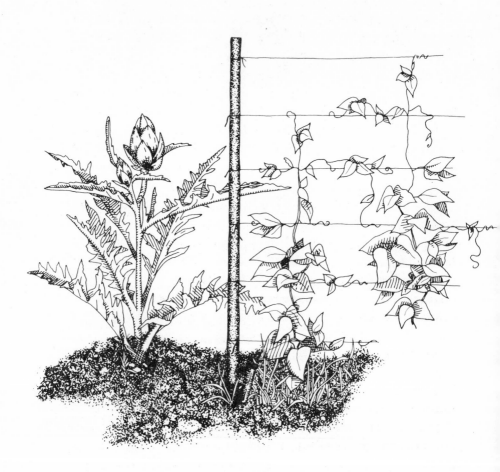

more expensive to buy a started plant or two than to start with seeds. Or, if you know someone who grows them, you may be able to trade something for a couple of plants, since artichoke plants multiply profusely on their own.

Artichokes grow on big, handsome plants with deeply cut leaves that are very ornamental. They like plenty of sunshine, but lots of humidity as well, and do especially well near the coast, where it is often foggy and rarely gets very hot in the summer. Plants should be set out in late spring in rich soil. A couple of feedings of manure tea or fish fertilizer, and a handful each of bone meal and wood ashes will get them off to a good start. After that, the most you can do is provide plenty of water. You can provide humidity for the plant as well by punching holes in one side of two or three large coffee cans, sinking them up to the rim in the soil with the holes facing the artichoke plant, and keeping them filled with water. The holes in the can release a slow, steady supply of water to the plants' roots, and evaporation of the water in the cans creates an island of humidity around the foliage.

Each plant will send up two or three artichokes in its first year; these should be cut and eaten when they are still tightly closed and fairly small. Always cut them with a sharp knife; never try to tear them off the plant or you will do great damage.

Mulch the plants fairly heavily in the fall with straw or grass clippings to keep the roots from freezing. The following spring, add some compost or manure around the roots, along with another handful of bone meal. Plants will yield more artichokes each year; a three-year-old plant may produce twenty or more between May and September. The new plants that sprout near the base of the mother plant can be dug up and given to friends, or used to increase your own supply.

Artichoke plants need a minimum of two square feet each,

and that's not counting room to walk between them. Since they are perennials, they must be placed in a permanent spot that doesn't get ploughed up every year.

Jerusalem Artichokes: No vegetable is so wrongly named as this one. Jerusalem artichokes are not from Jerusalem, and they aren't even remotely related to artichokes. They are native to North America, and are a second cousin of the common sunflower. Jerusalem artichokes, or sunchokes, have two outstanding virtues: they are as easy to grow as anything you'll ever plant, and they are completely starchless. Even though their texture is similar to potatoes, Jerusalem artichokes store their carbohydrates in the form of inulin rather than starch. They have almost no calories, and are therefore recommended for diabetics, and others who should limit their starch and calorie consumption.

The edible part of the Jerusalem artichokes grows underground, much like a potato. The plant that appears aboveground grows five or six feet tall, and, at the end of the summer, produces a small flower resembling a sunflower.

Plant Jerusalem artichoke tubers two inches deep and eight inches apart any time from late March to late May in the back of the garden where their tall foliage won't shade other plants. These plants like full sun but will do with less; in fact, they will grow almost anywhere, in almost any kind of soil. Fertilizer and fuss are wasted on them; they prefer neglect.

In October, after the foliage has died back, you can begin harvesting the tubers. You can either dig them all up at once, and store them in a cool, dark place, or you can leave them in the ground and harvest them as you need them. Save enough tubers to plant again in the spring.

It's not necessary to peel these gnarly little tubers; just boil them gently until they're tender, being careful not to overcook them. They can also be used sliced raw into salads.

ASPARAGUS: Once established, two dozen asparagus plants will provide enough for a small family each year for about twenty years. Asparagus needs full sun and lots of room—each plant needs at least two square feet, and an extra foot or two should be left on each side of the asparagus bed to provide for the spreading roots.

Asparagus is usually grown from two-year-old roots or crowns purchased from the nursery in late winter. It can be grown from seed if you are a patient soul, since it takes three years from seed till the time of first harvest. Even with two-year-old crowns, your first harvest will be a full year from the time you plant.

Because asparagus plants have massive root systems, often reaching six or eight feet into the soil, extra care must be taken in preparing the bed for them. The soil should be worked to a depth of at least two feet, and generous amounts of compost or manure worked in.

The bed should be along a fence or at the back of the garden, where the five-foot-tall summer asparagus ferns will not be in the way. It should also be clearly marked so that it is not accidently ploughed up.

To plant the roots, first remove six inches of soil from the bed and put it to one side. Then spread the roots out flat in the shape of a starfish. Cover them with about four inches of soil, and water thoroughly. Do not fertilize at this time, as the nitrogen in the fertilizer may cause the roots to rot before they can establish active growth. Leave the extra soil in a pile at the side of the bed, and gradually snuggle it up around the asparagus spears as they come up.

Don't despair if your asparagus doesn't come up for a month or two; it takes time for the roots to develop.

It will be tempting to eat those first spears; resist the temptation. They will grow into beautiful, feathery ferns which the plants need to build their strength for the following year. Keep the asparagus bed weeded, but don't cultivate more than an inch or two deep, so as not to disturb the roots. In the fall, cover with a layer of manure or mulch.

The following spring, your patience will be rewarded with a treat you may never have tasted: truly fresh asparagus. This spring, you must keep a close watch on your asparagus bed, for the spears mature in a matter of days, and, on a really good bed, daily harvests may be necessary. Cut them carefully at ground level or just below, taking care not to disturb the crowns. When the spears begin to look thin, stop cutting them, and let them grow into ferns. Never cut the ferns before they die back in the fall; they are an essential part of the plant's life cycle.

Fertilize the bed during the early part of its active growth season, and mulch it each fall.

"Mary Washington" is the best variety for this area, mainly because it is resistant to rust, a disease that affects asparagus plants in damp areas.

BASIL: An easily grown annual herb, basil comes in many forms. Bush basil, also known as French basil, is about a foot tall; larger varieties may be as tall as three feet. There is also an ornamental opal basil that makes a nice houseplant. The smaller varieties are generally stronger flavored.

It is a waste of money to buy bedding plants of basil, since it is easily grown from seed sown in the garden in late May. The weather must be warm for the seeds to germinate; there is no point in trying to hurry it by planting too soon. Basil likes full sun, but will do with half a day if that's all you have to offer. Once the plants are established, they should be thinned to six inches apart and fertilized lightly. The thinnings can be used in the kitchen.

When the plants are eight or ten inches high, you can start harvesting leaves as you need them. As the summer progresses, your plants will try to bloom and go to seed. Pick off the blossoms to prevent this; if you leave them to form seeds, the plant will think its work is done for the year and quit growing.

Basil is intolerant of soggy soil and will quickly develop root rot if it is kept too wet. This it the most common cause of failure in growing basil; the other common mistakes are planting it before the soil is warm enough, and planting it in soil that is not rich enough in humus and/or nitrogen.

BAY LEAVES: The bay leaves used in the kitchen come from a particular, slow-growing, frost-tender variety of laurel that resembles, but is not the same as, the common laurel hedge.

These plants are most commonly propogated by taking cuttings from established plants and rooting them. Young bay plants are often hard to find, since bay is not commonly grown here. Herbalists or nurseries specializing in herbs sometimes sell small plants.

If you find such a plant, the best course of action is to carefully install it in rich, well-drained soil in a large pot. It can be kept outdoors in a shady spot during the summer, and brought up on the porch where it will be protected from frost during the winter months. If you keep your house cool, it might be happy as an indoor plant. It should be repotted once a year, as it will grow six or eight feet tall, and may also require staking. If you prefer to keep it smaller, it can be pruned occasionally, and the leaves dried and stored in jars. Fresh leaves from the plant can also be used as you would use dry ones.

BEANS: There are many kinds of beans that consistently do well in Northwest gardens. All of the beans that are eaten in the pod, such as green beans, wax beans, and romanos, can be counted on for good harvests even for the beginning gardener. Beans that are grown for the bean itself rather than for the whole pod are grown here too; some gardeners manage to get crops of soy beans, kidney beans, and even limas. These latter beans generally take a longer growing season and more heat, however, so if you want to try growing them, it would be wise to start with a small quantity to see if they do well in your particular location and soil.

Edible-podded beans come in two forms: bush beans, which grow on two-and-a-half- or three-foot-high bushes, and pole beans, which grow six or eight feet tall and must have stakes to climb. Bush beans bear about two weeks earlier than pole beans, but don't bear as heavily. Pole beans require a little more space, but if a vote were taken on flavor, pole beans would most likely win over bush beans. Majority rule notwithstanding, it is a highly individual matter of preference, with every gardner defending the superiority of his or her chosen variety. And there are plenty of varieties of these beans to choose from: Kentucky Wonders, Oregon Blue Lake, several varieties of yellow wax beans, and romanos, which come in both bush and pole sorts.

Most of these beans are planted in May, after danger of frost is passed and the ground is fairly warm. If pole beans are planted, the poles should be set at planting time since once the beans get started they grow very fast. Many gardeners set three or four poles together like a teepee, and plant three or four beans at the base of each pole. Others plant them in rows and run string between stakes, as for peas, but if this method is used, the poles must be very strong and no more than four feet apart, for bean vines are much heavier than peas, and need more support. Pole beans may grow to be ten feet tall, but six-foot-high stakes will do, since when the bean vine reaches the top, it will bend over and start climbing back down.

All beans are legumes, and so have the ability to fix nitrogen from the air and store it in nodes in their roots. For this reason, they don't need high-nitrogen fertilizers, and in fact should not be given any since an excess of nitrogen will encourage leafy growth rather than beans. In gardens that have been organically enriched for several years, beans won't require any fertilizer, but would probably appreciate a handful of bone meal and some wood ashes. In new gardens, a light application of a low-nitrogen fertilizer at planting time will be sufficient.

Beans can be dropped in the furrow any old way, but a little extra attention will increase germination and save seeds. Look at a bean closely, and you will see a scar left on one side where the bean was attached to the pod it grew in. Plant the bean with this scar down, since the root grows down from there, and the two halves of the bean are pushed up out of the ground as it sprouts. Planting beans upside down or sideways makes them go to the extra work of turning themselves around in order to sprout, and may cause some of them to give up before they get out of the ground.

Beans like a lot of sun and a moderate amount of water. They are occasionally bothered by insects, most commonly aphids. If you keep a close watch on them you can check infestations before they become serious. Aphids can be hosed off and will usually expire before they can make it back to the plant. A bath of soapy water will get rid of them and presumably leave such a bad taste in their mouths that they won't want to come back. Aphid infestations most often start on the undersides of the leaves, so be sure to stop and look at them often.

Edible-podded beans should be picked when they are young and tender. They are best when they are about two-thirds the size of the ones you see in the market. Pole beans will start to bear in late August and continue bearing for a month or more. During this time, they should be picked every four days or so. Bush beans will bear earlier, and not for so long a time, but they, too, will benefit from frequent picking, since it pushes the plants along to keep trying to make mature seeds and so insure the survival of the species.

Beans grown for the beans themselves, such as limas, kidney beans, and soybeans should be grown like other beans, but should not be picked until the pods are fully developed. They should be left in a warm, airy place until they are thoroughly dry, or they can be dried in a food dehydrator. Then the beans can either be left in their pods or separated from them for winter storage.

A surplus of Kentucky Wonder beans can be dried for use like kidney beans, or, if picked when quite young, can be dried and later eaten, pod and all. If this latter is done, the dried beans should be brought to a boil in water, and then the water thrown away. They should then be simmered for several hours in water, with onions, garlic, and a little salt pork.

BEETS: There are many kinds of beets: small ones for pickling, large ones for winter storage, and beets with extra leaf growth for lovers of beet greens. All of them do well in our cool climate. Beets will tolerate light frost, so they can be planted in late

March. Aside from slugs, the only pests that afflict beets are root maggots, which can be discouraged by digging in plenty of well-rotted manure or compost at planting time, or by working a light dusting of Diazinon into the soil. Beet seeds are actually tiny fruits that contain several seeds, so even though you plant the seeds two inches apart, thinning will be necessary. If this is done when the beets are one or two inches in diameter, the thinnings can be steamed, along with their greens, for a nourishing treat. As the beets grow, you can occasionally pick a leaf or two from each plant for use in salads or to steam.

Several small plantings of beets at one-month intervals are advisable, since beets mature in about two months, and you will want a crop to mature at the end of the growing season for winter storage. The larger varieties are best for this purpose—Detroit Dark Red and German Lutz beets particularly. Beets are easy to store: they can be left in the ground if they are covered well enough to prevent freezing, or can be stored in a very cool, dark place where the air is fairly humid. Cut the tops off an inch or two above the beet, and don't trim the roots, or they will bleed. Stored in this way, they will keep for four or five months and will make wonderfully tasty and fragrant borscht on a cold winter day.

Beets are a good choice for gardeners with limited space, since they provide both greens and roots and will tolerate a little crowding.

BLUEBERRIES: Blueberries thrive in our moist, acidic soils and are pretty enough to use as an informal hedge in the yard. Hard work at planting time is a necessity, but once established, blueberries are pretty much pest-free, and will bear as much as fourteen quarts (a little over thirteen litres) of berries per plant for many years.

In late winter or early spring choose a sunny location, out of the way of rampaging children and other critters. Blueberry bushes will grow to about six feet in height and about three feet around, so they should be planted about four feet apart, in rows about five or six feet apart. They are not self-pollinating, so more than one variety must be planted to insure fruiting. Dig a trench bigger than you think is necessary; that is, at least three feet deep and two feet wide. Line the bottom of the trench with rotted manure and/or compost, and cover it with a three-inch layer of soil. Water this thoroughly, then set the blueberry plants so that they will be planted slightly deeper than they were at the nursery. Drainage is important to blueberries, so if your soil is heavy, mix in some peat moss as you fill in the trench, and as much more organic matter as you have available. When the trench is half full, and the plants are set, tamp the soil down firmly. Finish filling the trench, and tamp the soil again. Leave a saucer-shaped indentation at the base of each plant to collect rainwater. Soak thoroughly.

The only maintenance necessary for blueberry bushes is mulching or cultivating lightly to keep the weeds down around them. If, after several years, they become tangled or overcrowded, you may want to prune out old or damaged growth to make harvesting easier and to improve air circulation, but this won't be necessary every year. Some gardeners insist that blueberries should be given additional organic matter each year, but I have seen blueberry bushes that had been abandoned for many years bearing just as heavily as those that had been carefully pruned and fertilized.

Blueberries are ripe about a week after they turn blue, and should be picked every few days during the bearing season.

BOK CHOY: Also known as bok toy, this ancient oriental vegetable is well worth growing for use in salads or eating like celery even if you don't cook Chinese or Japanese dishes that call for it.

Bok choy grows and looks somewhat like celery, but matures much faster, and is much more prone to going to seed in warm weather. For this reason, it should be planted in a cool, shady corner of the garden, or planted late in the summer to harvest after the warm weather has passed. Thin seedlings to stand at least eight inches apart, and use the thinnings in the kitchen. To be at its best bok choy must grow fast, and so a monthly feeding of high-nitrogen fertilizer is needed unless the soil is very rich.

Bok choy should be harvested while the plants are smaller than those you see in the market; its flavor is better and more delicate when picked young.

BROCCOLI: Although broccoli takes up a fair amount of space, it is well worth growing, even in a small garden, because each plant produces many cuttings of one of the most nutritious, versatile vegetables known. It is a natural for our climate; it likes cool weather and will tolerate light frosts. Garden-fresh broccoli is good in salads, or served raw with a dip, as well as steamed, stir-fried, or thrown in the stewpot.

A first planting of broccoli can be made in late March or early April. Bedding plants can be put out at this time too, but since broccoli germinates easily and grows quickly, buying bedding plants is for the extravagant or the hurried. When plants are three inches tall, it is imperative that they be thinned or transplanted to stand at least eighteen inches apart. Broccoli will not tolerate crowding.

Successive plantings can be made up to the fifteenth of July.
Broccoli will do well with as little as four hours a day of
sun, but must have an ample supply of nitrogen to produce
abundantly. Monthly feedings of liquid fish fertilizer will serve
this purpose.

Broccoli is a member of the cabbage family, and vulnerable
to the same pests as cabbage. If cabbage is grown in the same
garden as broccoli, however, most of the cabbage-family pests
will go for the cabbages themselves, and leave the broccoli

alone. Even so, it is a good idea to discourage root maggots by surrounding broccoli seedlings with a handful of wood ashes or a light dusting of Diazinon worked into the soil. And if cabbage moths are seen hovering over the broccoli, steps should be taken to keep them from laying eggs on your plants. (These steps are described in the section on cabbage.)

Harvest broccoli while the heads are green and tight; don't let them bloom. Cut the main stalk three inches or so below the head. Side shoots will develop more, smaller heads, which should be harvested as soon as they are formed. If these side shoots are harvested while still young, and no flowers are allowed to develop, the bearing life of each broccoli plant can be extended for quite some time. A strong, healthy broccoli plant may bear for several months, often well into winter.

BRUSSELS SPROUTS: Another member of the cabbage family, brussels sprouts take up a lot of space, require lots of nitrogen, and are visited by root maggots and cabbage moths. But like other members of this family, the superiority of the flavor of fresh, home-grown sprouts is enough to warrant a little extra space and time. Brussels sprouts are also an exotic-looking plant that would be fun to look at even if you didn't eat any of it.

Brussels sprouts are slower to mature than other members of the family, and so a single spring planting is called for. If started from seed in early April, they will mature in September. When about three inches tall, they should be thinned to stand two feet apart, and their roots should be protected from root maggots with a handful of wood ashes or a light dusting of Diazinon worked into the soil. Monthly feedings with a high-nitrogen fertilizer, such as Alaska fish, are a good idea if your soil is not very rich. As the plants grow, each will develop a central, upright stalk, with leaves growing out of it in all directions. It is important to prune off all but the top cluster of leaves, so that the sprouts, which develop at the base of each leaf, will have room to grow, and so that the plant's energy is directed toward producing sprouts rather than leafy growth. Fend off cabbage moths by disguising the smell of the plants (see Cabbage).

Begin harvesting when the sprouts on the bottom of the stalk are an inch and a half in diameter. Cut them from the stalk with a sharp knife, being careful not to injure the stalk itself. If the little heads are kept cut as they reach this size, the plants will continue to produce well past first frost, and sometimes into December. Unless you are really passionate about brussels sprouts, one plant for each member of your family should be enough.

CABBAGE: There are many kinds of cabbage: savoy, Chinese, red or purple cabbage, and the traditional green heads. A little experimentation will teach you which of them is right for you. Among the green cabbages there are early, mid-season, and late varieties, so that you can have fresh coleslaw from late July until November. A single, well-grown cabbage is a large amount of food, so unless you want to make sauerkraut, you must be careful not to plant too many of the same variety at once, or you will find yourself with fifty pounds of cabbage to consume in one week. The later varieties can be stored for winter use if you have a root cellar or a cool garage or porch, but it is best not to plan on keeping them in storage for more than a month or six weeks.

The cultural requirements are the same for all varieties of cabbage: very moist, rich soil, plenty of lime, and at least a half a day of sun. Cabbages grown in poor or acidic soil, or deprived of water, will grow stemmy and will form poor, small heads.

Cabbages are easily grown from seed planted directly in the garden starting in early March. When seedlings are three inches tall, thin to stand two feet apart.

The real difficulty with cabbages is their extreme vulnerability to pests. In the spring, they are often attacked by root maggots. The symptoms of such an attack are not apparent until the damage has already been done. You will come out to your garden one morning, and find a cabbage plant collapsed on the ground. When you pull it up, you will find it has been eaten through, just under the ground, and completely severed from its root system. You will also probably find the culprit: a white, curled-up worm, no more than 1/4 inch long. Because root maggots are such a universal problem, it is best to prevent their damage rather than try to cure it; nothing short of a miracle will bring a cabbage plant back to life once a root maggot has found it.

There are two methods of prevention. The first is a commercial product called Diazinon. When setting out young plants, or while thinning, sprinkle a tablespoon of Diazinon dust around the roots of each plant, especially at the vulnerable spot just under the ground. If you are thinning plants already in the row, this means that you will have to dig up carefully each plant you intend to keep, apply the Diazinon, and replant. One application of Diazinon is usually sufficient to keep the root maggots away.

The second method of dealing with root maggots is the old-fashioned one: surround each plant with a small mound of wood ashes, and dig a cupful of ashes in the ground around the roots. The ashes will not kill the maggots, as

Diazinon does, but repels them. If a heavy rain washes the ashes away, you must replace them, at least until the first of July, when the danger of maggots is past.

The other cabbage-loving pest is also difficult to fight. It is the cabbage moth, a pretty little white thing that flutters over the garden, and almost invariably chooses the cabbage patch to lay its eggs in. These eggs then hatch out in the growing cabbage, and the larvae eat the cabbages. Constant vigilance is required to foil these beasties, because the cabbage will grow around and over them, and at harvest time you may cut open a head and find that the larvae have eaten half the inside of it.

The time to deal with this problem is the first time you see the white moth dancing over your garden. Again, there are two remedies: one, a chemical that kills the eggs, the other, an organic preventive measure. The pesticide to use is rotenone. Lightly dust the cabbage plants every ten days for as long as the moths are around, and oftener if the dust is washed away by rain. The organic method of prevention is, as usual, more time-consuming but less expensive. It requires that you concoct a mixture of onion juice and/or garlic juice and spray your cabbage plants with this smelly mixture to disguise their smell, thereby repelling the moths. The concoction can be made by boiling cut-up onions and garlic together in a pot of water, then straining the liquid into a spray bottle. It must be applied frequently as long as the moths are around. Companion plantings of strong-smelling herbs, onions, or garlic are also helpful.

If you succeed in fending off these pests, your labors will be well rewarded. There is a vast difference in taste between fresh, home-grown cabbage and what you've eaten from the store, and the plants themselves are impressively beautiful.

Always be optimistic about how large your cabbages will grow when you plant them, and leave at least two feet between plants. They *will* get that big—honest!

CANTALOUPE: New, earlier varieties of cantaloupe that have been developed in the last few years make this an easier fruit to grow than it used to be. Even the early varieties, however, insist on a full day of sun, rich soil, and plenty of water.

Cantaloupe can be started from seed outdoors in late May, or, better yet, from seeds started earlier indoors and planted out when the weather is warm. Even after planting out, cantaloupes appreciate a little extra encouragement: cover the young plants with Hotkaps or plastic to increase the warmth around them until early summer.

Cantaloupe grows like vining squashes, and so should be given four or five square feet for each group of three plants. Plenty of bone meal, or a high-phosphate fertilizer should be worked into the ground at planting time. Once fruit is set and starts to develop, it should be kept as dry as possible so that it won't rot. This can be accomplished by planting the seeds or young plants in a foot-wide depression, so that the vines will grow out to the surrounding soil. Then the plants can be watered without getting the cantaloupes wet by filling the depression.

Once several fruits have formed on each vine, subsequent blossoms should be picked off so that the plant will concentrate on maturing existing fruits.

Given a good supply of warmth and sun, cantaloupes will mature in late August or September. They are ripe when the stem separates easily from the fruit. If frost threatens before they are quite ripe, they can be picked early and ripened indoors, but the flavor is better if they ripen in the garden.

CARAWAY: The seeds of this plant are most commonly used in rye bread but are useful in other dishes as well. Oil from caraway plants is also used in certain liqueurs.

Caraway is a biennial plant that produces seeds during its second year of growth. It is best to plant caraway in a sunny, fairly dry spot during the summer, and mulch it in the fall so that its roots won't freeze during the winter. Then, the following summer, it will produce seeds. If it is planted in the spring, a few seeds may be produced the first year, but this is not always the case, and a much larger harvest is obtained by planting later in the summer and waiting a full year.

Caraway grows about thirty inches tall and looks somewhat like carrots. It would not be out of place in the back of a flower bed or as a border for the garden. It needn't be fertilized if the soil is very good; it is a hardy plant that self-sows readily if left to go to seed in the garden, and it will keep coming up year after year if a few plants are left in the ground each summer.

To harvest the seeds, cut the tops of the plants when the seeds are almost mature and store them loosely in a paper bag in a warm, dry place. When they are thoroughly dry, the seeds will fall to the bottom of the bag and can then be collected and stored in jars.

CARROTS: No garden is complete without carrots, nor is anyone's diet complete without the supply of vitamin A that carrots provide.

Carrots will grow in a wide variety of soils, so long as the soil is loose enough for the long roots to develop without running into hard-packed soil. Rotted compost or manure should be dug into the rows to the depth of one foot, and all stones and other debris removed.

Carrot seeds are tiny and somewhat difficult to handle.

They should be planted about a half-inch apart, and must be kept moist until they sprout. This is the key to successful carrot growing; the seeds are slow to germinate, and you will lose them if they dry out between the time you plant them and the time they come up.

Carrots are frost-hardy and so can be planted as early in the spring as the ground can be worked. However, they will germinate faster later in the spring when the ground is warmer, so if you tend to be impatient about waiting for things to sprout, you're better off to wait and plant them in May. Successive plantings of carrots can be made up until about the fifteenth of July.

When the carrots are about the size of your little finger, thin them to stand three inches apart. The thinnings are wonderful for table use, if you can refrain from eating them all while you're thinning. It's best to water thoroughly just before you do this job, so that the carrots are easier to pull.

Water the carrots deeply once a week or so. More frequent, shallow watering will keep the roots close to the surface of the soil, instead of encouraging them to grow longer roots that reach farther down for their sustenance. A mid-season feeding of fertilizer will encourage them, but it is not essential unless the soil is poor.

Carrots can be left in the ground for winter storage as long as the ground is not soggy. Cover them with a heavy mulch of straw, or a two-inch layer of soil to protect them from freezing weather. If you choose to take them up for storage, keep only sound, uninjured carrots, and pack them in boxes of moist sand in a cool place. Either way, they will keep for four or five months.

Wormy carrots are most often caused by the carrot rust fly, which lays its eggs on the carrots' foliage. The larvae that hatch out of these eggs burrow into the soil and eat the carrots. This pest is discouraged by digging plenty of wood ashes into the soil, or by disguising the smell of the carrots so that the flies can't find them. Companion plantings of strong-smelling plants, or the garlic/onion spray applied to carrots' foliage will control this problem if it occurs.

CATNIP: There are two kinds of catnip: one, a low-growing perennial with small blue flowers, and the other, an annual that grows about two feet tall and that has white flowers. The annual variety is the one cats go crazy for. The perennial catnip is used mainly as an ornamental plant and is not commonly available.

The biggest problem in growing catnip is cats. I know of no solution to this problem but to build a cat-proof fence around catnip plants, or to somehow hide them in a place your cat (or the neighbor's) doesn't frequent. Cats will roll on the plants, if not eat them, even when they are very young. There are cats that aren't very interested in catnip, and some that may not know about it. If these sorts of cats are around, you may be able to get some plants going long enough so that the plants get bigger than the cats and can then pretty well survive any feline attacks on them.

Annual catnip can be started from seed either indoors or in the garden when the soil is thoroughly warm. It needs fairly rich soil, but it is not fussy about drainage and will grow in damp spots. It likes a full day of sun, but will do with less. And if the cats leave any for you, the fresh or dried leaves make a soothing tea.

CAULIFLOWER: Another member of the cabbage family, cauliflower is a lover of cool weather, moist places, and rich soil. It can be grown successfully with as little as two hours of sunlight a day, and, in fact, prefers to avoid the hot afternoon sun.

Cauliflower can be started from seed in the very early spring, or in midsummer. Starting it in late spring is a chancy business, since in hot weather it will bolt and go to seed in a matter of days. If you do attempt to start cauliflower in the late spring, give it the shadiest spot in your garden, and hope for a cool summer.

Follow the directions for broccoli in growing cauliflower, and be sure to harvest the heads as soon as they form. Once you have cut the head, the plant is finished, so toss it into the compost pile and plant something else in its place.

Some people take up the big leaves around the heads and tie them, like a headscarf, over the cauliflower to keep it white. But the worst that can happen if you don't do this is that your cauliflower will turn slightly green. If you like your food colorful there's a purple variety of cauliflower (called Purple Head) which has the magical property of turning green when it is cooked.

CELERY: If you want to grow celery, be prepared to be its slave. Celery must grow rapidly to be good; if it grows too slowly, it will be stringy and strong-tasting. It is insistent on the best and richest of soils, plenty of water, and monthly feedings of high-nitrogen fertilizer. If you have a place to start seeds indoors, or a cold-frame or greenhouse, you can start celery from seed in early February. Otherwise, you'd best invest in bedding plants, since celery is frost-tender and takes too long to start from seed later in the spring. Even the tiny seedlings are demanding little things; they like feedings of manure tea or liquid fish fertilizer almost as soon as they've developed their first set of leaves.

When transplanting seedlings into the garden, plant them

ten inches apart in a row that is a depression about six inches deep and eight inches wide. During the four months that it takes them to grow, fill in this depression gradually with your very best compost.

Some gardeners harvest the outer stalks from each plant as they grow; others wait till the plant is mature and cut the whole stalk just above the ground. If the whole plant is cut, new growth will develop, but it will not be as large or as succulent as the first cutting.

Celery is not especially attractive to pests, except, of course, slugs and occasionally aphids.

If, after all this, your celery tastes bitter and stringy, let it sit there and go to seed, and you'll at least have some celery seed for your spice rack; you can also chop and dry the leafy parts of the plants for use in stews.

CHARD: If you like beet greens, you'll like chard. A distant relation of the beet family, chard is highly valued for its production of fresh greens long after fall frosts.

Chard can be started from seed anytime after the dead of winter, but since you will probably already have plenty of greens during the summer, the real value of chard is its ability to keep producing salad-quality greens late into the fall. For this reason, it makes sense to plant chard in rows vacated by early-maturing vegetables. Sown in mid-July, chard will be big enough to start harvesting by the end of August. Cut the outer leaves, and the plants will continue to produce new growth from the center.

Chard is virtually pest free, and it requires only an occasional feeding of high-nitrogen fertilizer to keep producing at its best.

CHERVIL: An easily grown annual herb, chervil is used much like

parsley as a garnish in soups and as an ingredient in salads. Seeds can be sown in early spring in a cold frame or in the house, or later, after danger of frost is passed, in the garden. Bedding plants are also commonly available in the spring.

Chervil will grow in almost any kind of soil, provided it is well watered, and it prefers a location that is shaded during the warmest part of the afternoon.

Leaves of chervil can be harvested as soon as the plants are large enough to tolerate a little pruning. Harvesting can continue all summer.

CHIVES: Chives are perennial plants that will thrive year after year with a minimum of care. Their delicate onion flavor has countless culinary uses, and their lavender flowers are useful in bouquets. The plants are pretty enough to serve as a border in your flower garden. Chives can be started from seed, but they're slow to germinate. And since the price of a package of seeds is not much less than the price of a bedding plant, you may opt for the latter. One plant is probably as much as you'll need, since chives grow in a clump that becomes bigger with each passing year.

Chives like a sunny place, lots of water, and an occasional feeding. If you buy a bedding plant, it will probably be pot-bound when you bring it home, so it's best to get it in the ground as soon as you can.

As soon as it is well established, you can cut some leaves for kitchen use. Always leave some growth to sustain the plant, but cut it often, for this encourages new growth. Once every three years or so, dig up the clump and divide it; give the divisions to your friends, or replant them in your own garden.

If you do the dividing in the fall, you may want to pot a small clump to keep in the kitchen window during the winter. Put it in a pot bigger than you think is necessary, since chives grow fast and have extensive root systems.

COLLARDS: The most common mistake in growing collard greens is growing too many. "Headless cabbage," as collards are called, are wonderful fried with a little bacon fat, or steamed with just salt and pepper. But a single package of seeds is too many for most families, unless you have a large freezer and are willing to spend the time to blanch and freeze all the collards you can't eat fresh. Collards can be started from seed as soon as the weather is warm; they will tolerate as much as a half day of shade and will grow in almost any kind of soil as long as they get plenty of water and enough nitrogen. They are magnificent looking plants, growing up to three feet tall with big, dark green leaves.

Start harvesting a few outer leaves from each plant when they are about a foot tall; they will continue to produce new growth until late summer, when they'll want to go to seed. Unless you plan to freeze some, two plants per person will be plenty.

CORN: Corn should be grown by two kinds of people: those with very large gardens, and those who love corn so much they are willing to give up a lot of precious space to these big, greedy plants. In order to insure pollination (without which there will be no kernels of corn), at least three rows of corn must be planted together. Each row should contain ten plants, planted eighteen inches apart. This means that you will need a minimum space of 4½ feet by 9 feet.

For our climate, the earliest varieties are best; those that take more than seventy days to mature are successful only if we have a good hot summer.

Corn should not be started until the soil has warmed to at least sixty degrees (15.5° Celsius) usually about the fifteenth of May. The seeds can be sprouted indoors between wet paper towels. When they have developed roots an inch long, they should be carefully planted out in the rows, eighteen inches apart and a full two inches deep. As the size of corn stalks indicates, they take a lot of nutrients from the soil. This means

that they will need very rich soil or an application of commercial fertilizer worked deeply into the soil before planting.

Corn is supposed to be "knee high by the fourth of July." That's a pretty variable measurement, of course, but if by July your corn isn't a couple of feet tall, you should probably give it another feeding of an all-purpose vegetable fertilizer. Work the fertilizer into the ground between the rows as you cultivate, and water it in well. Unless the weather is exceptionally dry, you will only need to water your corn two or three times during the growing season. When you water, give each plant a thorough soaking.

Each stalk of corn will develop side shoots, which should be cut off about two inches above the ground. These side shoots are usually vegetative growth, although sometimes they will try to produce an ear of corn or a second tassel. In hotter climates, they can be left on the plant, but here, where corn must be given every advantage to produce well, it's best to cut them off to direct the plant's energy to the main stalk. The occasional ear of corn that does develop on these side shoots is usually not completely pollinated anyway and so will be of poor quality. The side shoots should be cut early in July.

The soil between rows of corn should be kept well cultivated and loose during the early part of the growing season; but after the middle of July cultivation should stop, since the roots of the corn will have grown into the space between rows by then, and further cultivation might damage them. Walking between the rows of corn should also be avoided except when absolutely necessary.

Corn is ready to harvest about three weeks after the tassels on the top of the stalk begin to shed their pollen. To test for ripeness, pierce a kernel with your thumbnail. If the juice is clear, it is a little early yet. If it is milky, the corn is ready. And if the juice is thick and pasty, you've waited too long.

The sugars in corn turn to starch very soon after the ears are picked, so pick your corn just a few minutes before you're going to cook it.

Never grow corn in the same place two years in a row if you can avoid it because of the heavy demands it makes on the soil. Peas and beans are good crops to rotate with corn, since they help replenish the soil by fixing nitrogen from the air and storing it in their roots.

CRESS: Although true watercress won't grow in the vegetable garden, salad cress or curly cress will. Curly cress has a much nippier flavor than watercress, and so should be used sparingly in salads or as a garnish.

Cress is a small, fast-growing plant that will be ready to eat three weeks or a month after you plant it. Because you will use only a little at a time, it is best not to plant a whole package of seeds at once. A dozen seeds, planted in an area of a square foot, should be plenty to plant at one time.

Cress can also be grown in pots indoors all year round.

If you have a pond or stream, you might want to try true watercress. Plant the seeds about six inches above the water line. Leave some to go to seed, for watercress self-sows readily, and once established it will keep itself going indefinitely.

CUCUMBERS: Before you plant cucumbers, decide what you will be using them for. If you don't intend to make pickles, one or two vines of slicing cucumbers will be plenty for a small family, and since fresh cucumbers will need refrigeration to keep well, you'll want to avoid having too many ripe at once.

There are several kinds of slicing cucumbers: some that are guaranteed not to cause you to burp; some that are long and thin, such as Japanese or Armenian cucumbers; and lemon cucumbers, which grow on a somewhat smaller plant and are good for small-space gardens. (The cucumbers are lemon-shaped, not lemon-flavored.) If you want cucumbers for pickling, choose a variety whose size suits you. Some pickling cucumbers are very small and will fit easily into jars whole; others will be useful only for sliced pickles.

Cucumbers are fussy about two things: they must have warm, sunny weather, and if they aren't given an ample supply of water, the fruits will taste bitter.

Cucumbers won't germinate unless the soil is warm, and since they grow quickly, there's no need to rush planting them. The first of June is early enough to start seeds directly in the garden. Plant seeds an inch deep in groups of two or three, leaving three feet each way between groups. Cucumbers will be perfectly happy to sprawl along the ground, but if space is a problem, you may want to grow them on a fence, or train them to grow up stakes.

Harvest cucumbers as soon as they are big enough to eat or pickle. If you keep the fruits picked, the plants will continue to bear until frost.

DANDELIONS: I can see that smile creeping across your face as you come upon this common weed listed among respectable vegetables. But what other green can you sow outdoors on the first of March and harvest by the fifteenth of April? This is the time of year when you are most likely to yearn for fresh garden greens, and young dandelion leaves are as delicious as any greens that will ever come from your garden.

Sow the seeds (yes, you can buy dandelion seeds at most nurseries) as early in the spring as you care to venture outdoors. Well-cultivated, rich soil is best for fast growth that produces tasty greens. Keep an eye on the young plants, and pull them up before they start to flower. This is essential for two reasons: the greens become bitter once the plants flower, and if you make a fatal mistake of letting them go to seed, you will be pulling dandelions out of your garden for years to come. Dandelions have a long tap root; be sure to pull all of it out to prevent the plants from regenerating.

If, as I do, you already have an abundant supply of dandelions in your lawn, leaves from those plants can be harvested in the early spring too. But picking dandelion greens out of a wet lawn is a laborious job. It's much quicker and easier if they're all together in a row.

DILL: Even if you don't make pickles, dill is worth growing for its many other uses in the kitchen.

Dill is easily grown from seed sown in the garden in late May. The seeds are slow to germinate and must be kept damp until they come up. Once sprouted, however, dill is pest-free and requires no special care. You can start using dill leaves as soon as the plants are a foot high. When the plants begin to form seeds, cut them at the ground, tie them in bundles, and hang them upside down in a warm, shady place. Tie a paper bag or piece of cheesecloth over the heads to catch the seeds. When the plants have dried, shake all the seeds into the bag and store them in tight jars. Cut the leaves off the stalks, chop them, and store them in jars too.

For use in dill pickles, pick only the heads of dill; plants will often form second or third heads if heads are picked before seeds are formed.

EGGPLANT: A heat-loving vegetable that requires some coaxing to mature in our growing season, eggplant is worth any amount of fussing it takes to get mature fruit. Garden fresh

eggplant is, in fact, divine. Even if you think you don't like eggplant, try a plant or two, and once you have eaten them really fresh, you'll be addicted.

There are two basic types of eggplants: the big ones you see in the market most often, and a smaller Japanese variety that is picked when the fruits are about the size of large cucumbers. The Japanese varieties are the ones best suited for us, since they require a shorter growing season. Even so, they must be pampered a bit to mature unless we have an unusually warm summer.

Eggplants should be started from seed indoors in late March, and plants should be set out in the garden in late May, or bedding plants purchased for planting out. If the weather is still cool, eggplants can be given extra warmth by covering them with Hotkaps or clear plastic stretched over crouquet wickets. This greenhouse effect will speed their growth, but should be discontinued as soon as the weather gets really warm.

Eggplants should be watered deeply about once a week when they become well established, and an eye should be kept on them to prevent insect damage.

The lush, purple-veined plants will grow about two and a half feet in height and in width, so should be spaced two and a half or three feet apart in the row. Their delicate purple blossoms will begin to appear in early July, and fruits will mature toward the end of August or the first part of September. Fruits may hide under the leaves, so look closely for them. Overgrown eggplant may be bitter, so it is best to pick the fruits when they are no larger than eight inches in length.

In a good year, each plant will bear between ten and twenty fruits; if the weather has been cool and rainy, they may bear only a few.

Eggplant is a beautiful little bush, suitable for use in a sunny flower bed or border. It should be given the best of soil, rich with compost and/or manure, a handful of bone meal for each plant, and a midseason feeding of manure tea or fish fertilizer.

ENDIVE: If you think of endive as strong and bitter-tasting, you've never had young, fresh endive. This is a salad green that is truly not worth eating unless it's fresh.

Endive is frost-hardy, and so can be started in the very early spring, or in late summer for a fall crop that will keep bearing until very cold weather sets in. Escarole is a smooth-leaved variety of endive; ordinary endive is a low-growing plant with narrow, curly leaves.

Grow endive as you would other salad greens, making sure it has enough nitrogen to grow fast. Thin seedlings to twelve inches apart. For table use, you can pick the outer leaves of each plant as they grow, but be sure to harvest plants while they are young and tender. Endive will be tough and bitter if it is overly mature, or if it has grown too slowly.

FENNEL: For some odd reason, the growth of most vegetables is retarded if fennel is growing close by, so this herb should be planted away from the vegetable patch. Fennel comes in both annual and perennial varieties, both of which require plenty of sun and neutral or slightly alkaline soil.

Seeds of fennel can be sown in early spring, in soil to which plenty of lime has been added. The plants, which resemble dill, will grow to about three or four feet in height by the end of the summer.

Fennel requires no special care except for routine weeding during its growing season. When plants are well established, leaves may be cut for use in salads and soups. Later, when seeds have formed, the plants should be cut and allowed to dry thoroughly. The seeds can then be removed, stored in closed jars, and used for seasoning breads and candies.

GARDEN ROCKET: Also known as Mediterranean Salad, this is a leafy green plant of Italian origin. Its spicy leaves are used in salads, and would also make a nice cream soup.

Garden rocket is frost-hardy, and so can be planted early in the spring or late in the summer for fall use. Plants may go to seed during the hot part of the summer if they aren't protected from the hot afternoon sun. But if they do go to seed, they will self-sow readily, and new plants will sprout around the old ones.

Garden rocket should be treated just as you would lettuce: it needs well-cultivated soil, an ample supply of nitrogen, and constant moisture.

GARLIC: Companion planters say garlic is a must next to your cabbages to discourage the cabbage moth. A good planting of garlic is also guaranteed to keep werewolves out of your garden.

Buy whole garlic from your nursery or grocery store. Divide the cloves of garlic from each bulb, and plant each clove about three inches deep and three inches apart. Be sure to plant the cloves with their points up; as you can see if you look at the garlic bulb, the roots grow from the bottom.

Garlic planted in the fall or early winter will be ready for harvest in midsummer. During the summer, you can cut a leaf or two from each plant now and then for kitchen use.

When the tops die back, dig up all the bulbs, allowing their leaves to remain intact, and wash them thoroughly. Leave them in the sun until they're dry. Save some for replanting in the fall. Then, braid the rest together and hang them in your kitchen for winter use.

Some gardeners are currently very enthusiastic about elephant garlic, which is grown in the same way as ordinary garlic, but is several times larger. But the larger cloves of garlic are not as flavorful, and so you must use more of them. And, since they are larger plants, they will require more space in the garden.

HORSERADISH: If you can fall off a log, you can grow horseradish.

Buy roots at the garden store in late winter and plant them in rich, loose soil where the roots can grow unobstructed. Plant the roots about a foot apart, and mark the plantings so you won't confuse the horseradish with the weeds. Water them now and then during the summer, and begin harvesting roots in the fall. You can dig up only the side roots, and leave the plant in the ground, or dig up the whole thing and replant just a few of the roots. It's best to dig up just what you will use right away. The rest will keep well in the ground, and you can dig roots any time during the winter.

KALE, FLOWERING KALE: Another member of the cabbage family, kale is grown much like its relatives. It is a cool-weather crop that will need shade from the afternoon sun during the summer months. Like its relatives, it won't tolerate crowding, acid soil, or lack of nitrogen, and it will require lots of water. Curly green kale can be started from seed sown outdoors in the early spring. Thin seedlings to stand eighteen inches (45 cm) apart; eat the thinnings. When the plants are established, you can cut off the outer leaves for kitchen use and have a perpetual harvest for many weeks.

Flowering kale, or flowering cabbage, as it is sometimes called, is generally used as a winter substitute for flowers rather than for kitchen use. It doesn't truly flower, but derives its name from the highly decorative value of its colorful foliage. To grow it for winter decoration of your flower beds, start seeds in your garden in early August. Thin seedlings as you would curly kale and transplant to your flower beds any time after seedling are big enough to handle easily. These plants will live through the winter, but will go to seed in the spring. Curly green kale can also be planted in August for winter use in salads and as a cooked vegetable.

KOHLRABI: This is an odd-looking vegetable that produces

something that looks a little like a turnip, tastes a little like a cabbage, and grows aboveground.

Kohlrabi should be started from seed in the garden in the middle of April, or it can be sown anytime before the middle of August for later use. Kohlrabi is frost-hardy and matures from seed in about two months. When seedlings are four inches high, plants should be thinned to stand six inches apart. The thinnings can be steamed or used in salads. Kohlrabi will make do with less than a full day of sunshine, but requires fairly rich soil to keep it from getting tough and growing stemmy. It also needs an ample supply of water and an occasional feeding of manure tea or fish fertilizer to keep it growing fast, so that it will be crisp and mild.

Kohlrabi should be picked when it is about the size of a golf ball; the larger it gets, the stronger its flavor. Leaves of kohlrabi can be eaten too. Peeled and sliced, kohlrabi makes a nice hors d'oeuvre, and is also good in salads or in soups and stews.

LEEKS: These hardy, overgrown green onions can be grown year-round in the Pacific Northwest, except during unusually cold winters. They are very slow to mature, but are worth the wait just to have something fresh from your garden in mid-winter.

Plant seeds in the early spring for fall harvest, or in the early fall for a late spring harvest. Thin to stand three inches apart; use the thinnings as you would green onions.

Leeks won't do well without humus-rich soil, plenty of nitrogen, and a little protection from hot afternoon sun.

When you harvest leeks, use a trowel to dig under them before you try to pull them out; if you just pull on the tops they're likely to break. Each mature leek will have several small side shoots. Divide these carefully and replant them, and you can keep your leek bed going indefinitely without having to start over with seeds.

If you like Russian architecture, leave a leek or two in the ground and let them go to seed. The spire that holds the seeds is a beauty beyond description.

LETTUCE: There are upwards of a dozen different varieties of lettuce, but their cultural requirements are all the same: rich soil with lots of nitrogen, protection from hot afternoon sun during the summer, and vigilance against slugs.

Lettuce can be started from seed sown outdoors in early March, and succession plantings can be made through July. Spacing varies according to variety; head lettuce will obviously require more room than buttercrunch. Buying bedding plants of lettuce is a waste of money, since lettuce germinates quickly and easily, and the shock of transplanting nursery-grown lettuce at least partially offsets any headstart you might have gained.

If you want to try several different kinds of lettuce, for heaven's sake don't plant a whole package of seeds of each kind. Sow just a few of each kind in the spring, and save the rest for gradual use in succession plantings.

You can harvest the outer leaves of each lettuce plant as they grow rather than pulling up the plant. Head lettuce can be cut at ground level, and will produce new growth, but the second growth will be smaller than the first. After several weeks of cuttings, one of two things will happen: either your lettuce plants will just wear out, or they will bolt and go to seed. In either case, this is the time to pull them out and plant something else.

Some kinds of lettuce are more prone to going to seed than

others, but generally speaking, the problem of bolting can be minimized by growing lettuce in a spot where it is shaded during the afternoon, and keeping the plants well fed, watered, and happy.

MARJORAM: A perennial herb that tastes like a mild form of oregano, marjoram is generally grown from started plants bought from the nursery or herbalist.

Like most perennial herbs, marjoram's flavor is stronger if it has to struggle a little for its survival. Ideally, it should be given good, enriched soil to start with, and should not be fertilized at all. An annual application of a little manure or compost around the base of the plant is really all that's needed. Marjoram will, however, grow in moderately poor soil if it is given a little fish fertilizer or manure tea now and then.

One plant is more than enough for family gardens, since the plant grows and spreads with each passing year, and will eventually become a two- or three-foot-wide bush. Plants can be set out at any time during the growing season and left in the ground through the winter with a light mulch around the base of the plants so that the roots don't freeze.

Leaves can be harvested year-round too; just cut what you need as you need it.

MINT: In addition to the common spearmint and peppermint, there are all sorts of exotic mints that are just as easy to grow: lemon mint, pineapple mint, apple mint, and even basil mint spread rapidly from started plants.

Since one plant of each sort of mint is as much as you'll need, buying bedding plants is justified unless you particularly want to try growing them from seed. Mints need good treatment in the form of good soil and lots of moisture to get going, but once established are better neglected than fussed over. They will

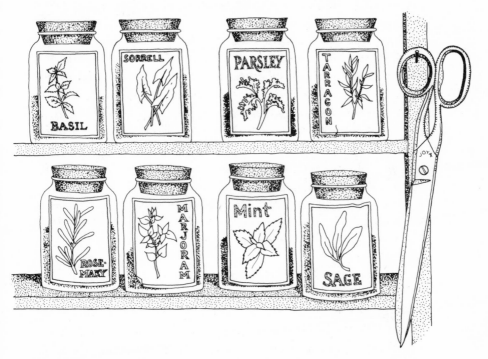

easily take over the garden, since they spread by very hardy, persistent root growth. Ploughing and cultivating won't get rid of them once they've gotten started; cutting up the mint roots only makes them multiply faster. For this reason, they ought to be planted in some out-of-the-way place where their aggressive habits will not disburb other plants.

Mints are not fussy about sunlight; they will grow equally well in sun or half-shade. Nor do they need any winter protection; they will, in fact, live through even our coldest winters and leaves can be harvested in midwinter.

MUSTARD GREENS: No crop produces greater quantities of greens faster than mustard greens. They are ready to eat six weeks after planting seeds. Their only fault is that they become very strong tasting when they are large, and they will flower and go to seed as soon as the weather gets warm.

Plant mustard greens in the early spring for harvest in June, or in mid-August for a fall harvest. A light feeding of high-nitrogen fertilizer is all they'll need during the growing season. Begin harvesting leaves when they are four inches across; break off outer leaves from each plant, and they will continue to produce.

Don't plant a whole package of seeds unless you're really crazy about mustard greens; half a package in the spring, and half a package again in August will be plenty. The late planting will last well past first frost. It takes a hard freeze to stop mustard greens, and the early frosts are said to improve their flavor.

ONIONS: Although our growing season is a little short for growing onions from seed, a good crop can be easily grown from onion sets, or seed onions, planted in the very early spring.

Onions sets are sold by the pound at nurseries and garden stores, and can be grown to maturity for large bulb onions or harvested early for use as green onions. It is more economical to grow green onions from seed, of course, and since green onions require a much shorter growing season, it is a little extravagant to use onion sets for this purpose. You may also be lucky enough to find started plants of Walla Walla sweet onions at your nursery; if you do, don't pass them up.

For bulb onions, plant onion sets or started plants four or five inches apart about the first of March. While they are growing they require plenty of water and an occasional feeding of a balanced fertilizer.

In the unlikely event that your onions are attacked by root

maggots of some kind, plant a crop of radishes between them. The root maggots will prefer radishes to onions, and when the radishes have been thoroughly infested, pull them out and discard them.

In September when onions begin to mature, bend the tops of the plants over to the ground. This need not be done gently; you can knock them all over with the back of a rake. Leave them in the ground for two or three days after you do this. Then pull them out and lay them on newspapers in a warm, dry place until they are thoroughly dry and the tops have completely withered and turned brown. It is essential that onions be well dried before they are stored, or they will not keep properly. This generally takes about ten days. After this curing process is complete and the skins of the onions are dry and papery, the onions can be braided by their tops, like garlic, and the braids hung in a cool dark place; or the tops can be cut off, and the onions stored in open containers (such as slatted crates or mesh bags).

Egyptian or "Walking" Onions: Some of the seed catalogues carry bulbs of these odd plants. Grown from bulbs planted in the fall, Egyptian onions are perennial plants that produce small onions on the top of a tall stalk. As the planted bulb grows from year to year, the onions produced on the top of the stalk grow larger, too. They can be harvested for table use, or replanted to start new plants.

Green Onions or Scallions: Green onions require very rich soil, but can do with as little as four hours of sun a day. Lacking good soil, they will come up like spindly grass, so be sure to save some of your best compost for them.

Green onions can be planted in the early spring. Since they

don't keep very well, it's best to plant a few at a time to keep a steady supply coming in. Green onions can also be planted in the late fall for a crop in the following March.

OREGANO: Like most other perennial herbs, oregano is usually propagated by taking cuttings or divisions from existing plants. It can be started from seed, but since one plant will provide as much oregano as you could possibly want and more, it is usually just as economical to buy a small plant as it is to buy a package of seeds.

Oregano is a woody, little shrub that produces best when it is not over-fertilized. Too rich a soil or too much fertilizer will cause the oregano to be less flavorful. This is not to say that oregano can take a lot of abuse; it should be planted out in good soil, with some manure or compost dug into it to give it a good start and help it establish itself. When plants are first set out, they should also be watered frequently until they are thoroughly settled.

Like most other herbs, oregano is a sun-lover, but will manage with just half a day of sun if it must. A light mulch during winter to protect its roots from freezing is required, and, after the plant has been in the garden for two or three years, it should be dug up and divided. The divisions can then be planted back in the garden where they will have a little more space to sprawl, or they can be given to friends.

Oregano leaves can be cut as they are needed once the plant is established.

PARSLEY: The most frustrating part of growing parsley is waiting for the seeds to sprout; parsley is very slow to germinate, and it may not come up for a month.

Aside from that, however, parsley is easy to grow—it's not fussy about soil, and can get by on a half-day of sun. It is pest-free except for an occasional slug passing through, and although it will appreciate a little fertilizer now and then, even that is not essential.

You can begin cutting parsley as soon as the plants are well established; each plant will continue to produce new leaves all year and into the next spring. Then, when the weather warms up, plants will go to seed, and should be pulled out and discarded. Parsley plants can also be potted and brought indoors in the fall, but must have a deep pot to accommodate their rather long taproot.

In addition to common parsley, there are several larger varieties worth trying: parsnip-rooted or Hamburg parsley, mitsuba, a perennial Japanese parsley, and Giant Italian parsley, which grows three feet tall and can be eaten like celery.

PARSNIPS: The real work of growing parsnips is in the soil preparation; some parsnips may be fifteen inches long, so the soil must be loose and fertile to at least that depth.

Parsnips grow like carrots and beets but take a lot longer. If planted in early May, they will be mature in September or early October. They are big plants and should be thinned to stand a minimum of six inches apart, and they must have an adequate supply of water throughout the growing season, or they will become woody and fibrous. Unless the soil is very poor, they won't need to be fed while they're growing, and they are about as pest-free as anything you will ever grow. Parsnips can be stored in a cool, dark place during the winter, or left in the ground with a mulch of straw over them.

Parsnips can also be planted in the early fall for a late spring crop.

PEAS: Our long periods of damp, cool weather make peas thrive; if you're not careful and plant too many, you could spend your whole summer sitting on the front steps shelling peas.

Plant peas anytime after the first of March. You can speed up germination by soaking the seeds for twenty-four hours before planting, but that's not essential. Plant the seeds an inch deep and two inches apart; thin plants to stand about four inches apart. Keep the seeds moist until they're up, and provide string for them to climb as soon as they are a couple of inches high.

It's best to set stakes for peas before you plant them so that you don't disturb the plants after they've become established. Pea stakes should be sturdy, deeply set, and about four or five feet apart.

In reasonably good soil, peas will not need any fertilizer, since they can fix nitrogen from the air and store it in nodes in their roots for use as they need it.

As soon as they begin to bloom, start keeping a close watch on them; the pods will mature very quickly and should be picked while young and tender both for the best flavor and to encourage more production.

Snow peas, or edible pod peas, should be harvested as soon as the pods are three inches long. If left to grow larger, the pods will become stringy and tough. Since peas grow so fast, you will have to pick snow peas every other day for as long as your plants are bearing.

Peas planted in the early spring will finish bearing by the middle of July. At that time, the vines should be cut off at the ground and tossed in the compost box. Always leave the roots of pea vines in the ground, since the nodes of nitrogen stored on them will benefit the soil. After the vines have been cut, you can replant peas for a fall crop, or plant something else in the same space. Peas planted for a fall harvest won't bear as heavily as spring peas, and by the time you finish harvesting your spring planting you may not want to look at another pea for at least a year anyway.

PEPPERS: These sun-loving plants demand the best soil you have, at least eight hours a day of sun, and plenty of water. In return for these considerations, they will give you one of the prettiest and most satisfying vegetables in the garden.

Both green peppers and smaller hot peppers like jalapeños are frost-tender and require a longer growing season than we have, so seeds should be started indoors in mid-March for planting out about the first of May, or plants should be purchased from a nursery. The first of May is an approximate date for planting out peppers; if it's still chilly, you may as well wait a week or two until the ground is thoroughly warmed up.

Green peppers should be set two-and-a-half feet apart; jalapeños or other small, hot peppers should be a foot apart.

Leaf-munching insects may bother pepper plants when they are young; they can be controlled with rotenone. Insect tastes are offended by the piquancy of the peppers themselves, however, and so no one but you will eat your peppers. In fact, some gardeners steep hot peppers in boiling water and use the peppery water as a spray to repel insects on other plants.

Peppers need a fertilizer that is high in phosphorus to produce fruit. Too much nitrogen and not enough phosphorus will encourage lots of leafy growth, but no peppers. An application of bone meal or a good, high-phosphate vegetable fertilizer worked into the soil before you set the plants out will supply the needed phosphorus.

POTATOES: Potatoes take up a lot of space, so unless you have a very large garden you won't be able to grow a full year's supply.

Even so it's worth it to grow some plants just to have new potatoes for a few meals in the late summer and fall.

Potatoes can be planted anytime after the middle of March, but there's no real hurry; the fifteenth of May is soon enough to give them time to mature before fall. Potatoes should not be planted for two weeks after your garden has been ploughed or rototilled, because the soil micro-organisms are very active then, and are likely to go to work on your seed potatoes, causing them to rot rather than sprout. If you have grown a winter cover crop on your garden, you should wait even longer, about three weeks, to give the cover crop plenty of time to decompose.

Potatoes are not terribly fussy about soil and will be one of the better crops in new gardens. They prefer acid soil, so no lime should be applied where they will grow. An excess of nitrogen is also damaging to potatoes; it may cause excessive foliage growth and little tuber growth, and may also cause potatoes to rot. For this reason, manure and compost should not be worked into the soil before planting. The best practice is to dig these in in the fall, but if this has not been done, the next best course of action is to use a low-nitrogen fertilizer at planting time, or work in some bone meal and wood ashes before planting.

Seed potatotes can be purchased at nurseries in the early spring; don't use potatoes from the grocery store, because they have probably been treated with a chemical that inhibits sprouting. Cut up seed potatoes so that there are at least two eyes on each piece, then let them dry for a couple of days. Plant the pieces eighteen inches apart in rows two feet apart. To plant, set the seed potatoes on top of the ground, then rake a mound of soil over them. As the potato plants grow, keep raking the soil up around them so that the mound of soil around each plant gets larger and larger. This will provide the potatoes with plenty of loose soil to grow in, and will make them easier to dig at the end of the season. If you don't do this, your potatoes will be down deep in the soil, and the work of digging them will be much harder.

Over the years, gardeners have come up with a thousand ways to provide potatoes with loose soil, and to minimize the work of digging them. Some people grow potatoes in large garbage cans, starting them near the bottom and gradually filling the cans with dirt as the plants grow. Others start by planting potatoes in an old tire, then stack more old tires on top of it and fill them with dirt as the season progresses.

Give potatoes plenty of water while they're growing, but don't let the ground get soggy or hard-packed.

For a real treat, dig a few potatoes in mid-July, when they're the size of large walnuts, and boil them gently for a few minutes and serve them with butter and fresh parsley. Yum!

Potatoes to be stored for winter should not be dug up until the vines have completely died back and the skins of the potatoes are cured. The skins should not slip away from the potatoes when you rub them with your hand. Store only sound, uninjured potatoes, since injuries will make them vulnerable to decay. Keep them in a cool dark place, and be sure to leave enough for next spring's planting, no matter how good they taste.

PUMPKINS: Big pumpkins are best for Halloween carving, and smaller ones are best for pies, freezing, and eating like squash.

Plant pumpkin seeds in mid-May, when the weather has thoroughly warmed up. Pumpkin vines need a lot of room;

allow four square feet for each group of three seeds, and be prepared to beat back the invasion when the vines get big later in the summer. As you might imagine, pumpkins require prodigious amounts of water and an ample supply of fertilizer unless your soil is very good.

When pumpkins form, put a piece of board under each one to keep it dry on the underside, and to keep it away from slugs.

If you want to grow mammoth pumpkins, choose seeds advertised for their size, and plant them in plenty of manure or compost. Water and fertilize them often, and pinch off all but one pumpkin on each vine.

Harvest pumpkins when their skins are tough and the vines begin to die back. A light frost won't hurt them, but they should be brought in before the weather gets really cold. If you plan to store them, don't wash them, and keep them in a dark, cool place that is dry and well ventilated.

RADISHES: Radishes are so easy and fast to grow they're a good crop to let your children be in charge of. The most common mistakes in growing radishes is planting them too soon. If you want homegrown salad, wait until your lettuce is half grown to plant radishes; otherwise, your radishes will have come and gone before your lettuce is ready to eat. Radishes go from seed to harvest in about twenty-eight days.

It is generally unnecessary to reserve a row for radishes; they can be tucked into a corner, or scattered among flowers, or they can be sown along with a slow-germinating vegetable like parsley. The parsley will just be coming up when you harvest the radishes.

The second most common mistake in radish-growing is planting too many at once; empty the package of seeds into a small jar, and plant just a few every week throughout the spring and summer. Summer plantings of radishes should be made in shady places, since hot weather will cause them to go to seed.

If root maggots bother your radishes, sprinkle a little Diazinon around the seeds when you plant them, or work in a handful of wood ashes to repel the maggots.

In addition to the classic red radishes there are many interesting varieties of big white ones; they are slower to mature, but have a much wider variety of uses. They can be pickled (the Japanese pickle them with rice vinegar rather than apple cider vinegar), breaded and fried, used as a substitute for water chestnuts, or sliced into salads.

ROSEMARY: This perennial herb is more tender than some of the others, and it is important that it be heavily mulched during the winter to protect it from freezing, especially for small young plants.

Rosemary should be treated like other perennial herbs; that is, it should be planted out in good, organically enriched soil, and not fertilized more than once a year. It likes full sun but will do with less if necessary. A vigorous rosemary plant will, in three or four years, grow into a small shrub that is attractive enough to be included in a flower border or along a walkway.

Though rosemary can be started from seed, the usual practice is to start with a small bedding plant, since one plant is as many as you'll need. When the plant becomes very large, after three or four years, it can be dug up and divided if it becomes crowded.

RHUBARB: Started from root divisions in either the spring or the fall, rhubarb is a perennial that will keep you supplied with the makings of pie and sauce for the rest of your life.

Rhubarb plants are happy in almost any kind of soil, as long as they get plenty of sun. Buy a root division from a nursery or from a friend who has established plants. Each root division should have one or two buds on it; plant it in loose, well-worked soil with the buds just above the ground. Give each plant at least three square feet of space. Water well when you set out the root, and keep it watered until it's established.

After that, you can neglect your rhubarb until it produces enough stalks for a pie or two. If you plant in the fall, you should have enough to harvest by the following spring; if you plant in the spring, you may have to wait until the following spring. After that, you will be able to harvest stalks from your plants three or four times during each growing season.

Once every five years, dig up your plants and cut the roots into sections. This can be done with a sharp knife, or if the roots are very large, with an axe. Replant the root divisions, give them to friends, or discard them. Use only the stalks from your plants; the leaves are poisonous.

Rhubarb is pest-free, an aggressive enough grower to triumph over most weeds, and hardy enough to live through even the most severe winters.

Some manure or compost dug into the soil at planting time will get the plants off to a good start, but after that you probably won't need to fertilize again until you dig them up to divide the roots.

RUTABAGAS: A root vegetable similar to turnips, rutabagas are distinguished by their yellow flesh, their sweetness, and their good keeping quality. They are a wonderful addition to soups and curries on cold winter days, and can also be boiled and mashed like potatoes. Because their outstanding virtue is their ability to keep through the winter, the best use for rutabagas is as a fall crop. Plant them in early or mid-July, just as you would beets or turnips. Thin the plants while young to six or eight inches apart.

In the fall, let them stay in the ground through a couple of light frosts. Then, either leave them in the ground and mulch them heavily so they won't freeze, or dig them all up, cut off the tops a couple of inches above the roots, and store them in slatted boxes in a cool, dry, dark place. Don't wash them before you put them away; they need to be dry to keep well.

SAGE: The essential ingredient in your Thanksgiving turkey stuffing is easy to grow either from seed or from bedding plants. Choose a sunny spot that will accommodate the sprawling habits of this two-foot-high perennial. If you plant seeds, keep them damp until they've germinated; if you start with a bedding plant, give it a good watering and some fish fertilizer when you set it out. If you're starting from seeds, you'll want to keep only one or two sage plants; the rest can be given to friends, or pulled and discarded.

Once your sage is well established, you can harvest leaves as needed. But since sage is a pretty aggressive grower, you may also want to give your plant a good haircut now and then to keep it from taking up more than its share of space. Do this just before it blooms and hang the prunings in a dry place for a few days till they're dry, then chop them and store them in jars.

An annual feeding of a balanced fertilizer, or the addition of a little compost or manure around the base of the plant is all sage needs; over-fertilizing or over-watering will tend to weaken the flavor of the leaves.

SALSIFY: This oddity produces a long, white root that tastes vaguely like oysters, and is otherwise known as oysterplant. Its leaves look like the leaves of leeks; they are long and flat and about eighteen inches tall.

Salsify seeds should be sown in mid-April in soil that has been worked deeply to accommodate their long roots. Plants should be thinned to stand five inches apart. Full sun, good soil and an occasional watering are all they'll need from then on.

Salsify should be left in the ground until after the first light frosts as this improves their flavor. They can then be cooked in any way that you would cook potatoes. Those not used right away can be left in the ground and mulched so they won't freeze, or taken up and stored as you would carrots.

SAVORY: Summer savory is an annual plant with a somewhat milder flavor than its perennial cousin, winter savory. Both are used in salads, meat dishes, soups, stews, and with poultry.

Summer savory is easily started from seed in late May, or sown earlier indoors and plants set out when the weather is warm. Leaves of summer savory can be used as soon as the plants are large enough to tolerate some pruning. When the plants bloom, the savory will be strongest; it can be brought indoors and dried at this point for use through the winter.

Winter savory can also be started from seed, but since one plant is plenty, the price of a bedding plant may be justified. Winter savory needs a mulch to protect it from winter freezing, but otherwise it can be treated the same as summer savory. Both like full sun, moderately good soil, and plenty of water.

SHALLOTS: These delicate little members of the onion family are a cross in flavor between scallions and garlic, and are much prized by gourmet cooks.

Like garlic, shallots multiply from a single bulb. Divide and plant shallots as you would garlic, so that each clove is planted point up. This should be done in early winter, at the same time that garlic is planted. Rich soil, full sun, and a little water are all they'll need from then on. Shallots will be ready to harvest in late summer or early fall when the tops die back. When this happens, pull them up and let them dry either in the sun or in a warm, airy place indoors. They can then either be stored in mesh bags in a dark, dry place, or braided like garlic and hung up in the kitchen.

SPINACH: Once you've eaten fresh, homegrown spinach raw in a salad, you may never want to eat it cooked again. It is superior to lettuce both in flavor and nutritive value, and both of those values are seriously compromised by cooking.

Spinach grows very fast from seeds sown in cool weather; it matures in about seven weeks. True spinach is intolerant of hot weather, and will go to seed rather than produce leaves if it's too warm, but there is a "hot weather spinach," New Zealand spinach, that can be grown during the summer. It is not as flavorful as true spinach, though, and is better cooked than raw.

Plant seeds of true spinach either in the early spring or in the early fall in extra-rich, moist soil. Thin plants to four inches apart and harvest outer leaves as soon as plants are well established. New growth will continue to develop until the weather gets warm, or until it frosts. When plants start to send up a stalk in the center for seeds, harvest the whole plant. If it looks like the summer is going to be cool, you can try for a summer crop of true spinach if you have a shady place for it. Otherwise, try the New Zealand variety during the warm months.

Unfortunately, spinach is a delicacy appreciated by slugs and insects as much as by humans, so you will have to patrol your spinach bed daily to fend off all manner of competitors.

Slugs are generally the worst threat, especially to very young plants; be prepared to use every weapon in your arsenal of slug-control tactics to keep them at bay.

SQUASH: This venerable family includes cucumbers and zucchini, hubbards and crooknecks, acorn squashes and butternuts. All of them are notorious for taking up a lot of space, requiring a lot of water, and generally getting rowdy and taking over the garden before the summer is over. Cucumbers are the only members of this family that have any manners at all; see

the section on them for more information on their special habits.

The two main kinds of squash are summer squashes—such as zucchini and summer crookneck, which are picked when quite immature and used fresh—and winter squashes, which are left to mature on the vine and kept in storage through the winter.

A single leaf of most squash plants will be a foot across, and the vines may grow to be eight or ten feet long. Some varieties grow as bushes rather than producing long, trailing vines, but even the bush varieties are so large that they require four square feet of space. Because of their size, squashes are not grown in rows, but planted in groups of three in saucerlike depressions several feet apart each way.

In each of these depressions, plenty of manure or compost should be dug in, along with two handfuls each of bone meal and wood ashes. If these are not available two handfuls of vegetable fertilizer should be dug in instead. Six or eight squash seeds can be planted in each of these depressions; the plants should then be thinned to leave the three strongest vines.

Most squashes are frost-tender, so planting should not be started until danger of frost is passed and the soil is thoroughly warm. Bush sorts should be planted separately from vining squashes, since if they are together you won't be able to wade through all those vines to harvest the zucchini.

Squash plants are sun-lovers, and so should be planted in full sunlight, and, since they produce such large fruits, they will need an ample supply of water throughout the growing season.

Summer squashes should be kept picked to encourage plants to continue bearing; if they are allowed to mature, the plants will have succeeded in their mission to produce seeds and may consider their life's work complete.

Winter squashes should be left on the vine until the vines begin to die back. They can be left in the garden through the first light frosts, as this is said to improve their flavor, but should be brought in before the weather gets really cold.

Winter squashes will keep well in a dry, cool place. Don't wash them before you put them away; they must be dry to keep well. Handle them carefully, since bruised spots or injuries will cause them to rot in storage.

STRAWBERRIES: There are hundreds of varieties of strawberries, each with special uses. There are varieties developed especially for freezing, some developed to have extra large berries that look appealing to buyers in the market, some with exceptionally high sugar content for making jams and jellies, and some, called everbearing, that produce fruit throughout the entire summer rather than bearing just once in June.

Usually, however, only a few of these varieties are available for the home gardener to choose from. The choice between everbearing varieties and varieties that bear only once is the first decision to make. If you have room for only a few plants, everbearing strawberries may be frustrating, since you may never have enough berries at one time to make jam or preserves. And in a larger plot, you may get tired of picking strawberries all summer. But if you are devoted to the pursuit of fresh strawberries, the everbearing varieties are for you.

Buy strawberry plants in the early spring, either from a nursery, or from one of the seed catalogues. When you get them, they will look hopelessly bedraggled and not very promising, but don't let that discourage you.

There are several ways of planting them, but the essential

factor is sun: strawberries need at least eight hours of it a day. They will survive in almost any kind of soil, but will produce more heavily if the soil is enriched with manure and compost and some bone meal to supply them with the phosphorus they'll need to produce fruit. Strawberries prefer acid soil, so don't add lime to the strawberry bed. Good drainage is important to them too. They need a lot of water during their growing season, but they don't like to be soggy.

You can plant strawberries in rows eighteen inches apart, or you can plant them closer together in beds three or four feet wide, so that they will form a solid mat of growth over the whole bed. If you plant in these wider beds, be sure the bed is not so wide that you can't reach across to pick the berries. Where space is limited, strawberries can be grown in barrels with holes cut in the sides. The holes should be about an inch in diameter, and cut ten inches apart each way all around the barrel. The barrel is then filled with good soil to the depth of the first row of holes, and the berry plants inserted in the holes so that their roots are inside the barrel, and the new growth protrudes from the holes. Then the barrel is filled with dirt to the next row of holes, and the process repeated until the barrel is full. Unless the barrel is turned around often, the plants on the north side won't get enough sun to produce fruit, so if you try this, you may want to mount the barrel on some kind of swivel so that it's easy to turn, or just plant the side of the barrel that will get the most sun.

Strawberries reproduce themselves by runners that grow from the center of each plant. Each runner will sprout one or more new plants, which, if left to their own devices, will grow roots and establish themselves in your strawberry bed. During the bearing season, it's best to cut off all of these runners to keep the mother plant's energy focused on producing fruit. But after the bearing season is over, you may want to let some of these runners develop new plants to increase your supply, or to replace plants that didn't perform well. Once the daughter plants along the runners have developed a few roots, you can cut them off the runner and plant them where you want them to grow. Use only the daughter plants from the best of your mother plants, and you can increase the productivity of your patch.

The productive life of a strawberry plant is three or four years, so the process of replacing plants should be a continuous one.

The most troublesome pests around strawberry plants are the birds that take one annoying bite out of each berry; they can be foiled by covering the bed with chicken wire or nylon or plastic netting sold at nurseries for this purpose.

Feed strawberry beds each spring with a high-phosphate fertilizer, or with some manure or compost and some bone meal.

TOMATOES: Undisputed as queen of the vegetable garden, tomatoes have an undeserved reputation for being difficult to grow. Given a full day of sun, reasonably good soil, and a minimum of care, tomatoes will produce abundantly here in the Pacific Northwest. The only limitation is on the varieties of tomatoes we can grow: large, late-bearing varieties like beefsteak tomatoes will do well here only during a good hot summer. But smaller, early tomatoes do just fine.

Our growing season isn't long enough to allow for planting tomato seeds outdoors, so seeds should be started indoors in March, or bedding plants can be purchased from a nursery.

The sunny spot where tomato plants will grow should be well perpared several days before planting time to allow it to

settle. Generous amounts of manure or compost, and a good high-phosphate fertilizer should be worked into the soil.

Tomato plants should be set out after danger of frost is passed and the soil has warmed up—usually about the middle of May. Plants should be set three feet apart each way and given an application of liquid fish fertilizer or transplanting solution when they are set out.

Stakes should be provided for tomatoes, and should be set either before the plants are set out, or very soon after. If you wait until the plants are large to stake them, you will be driving the stakes through their roots, and the plants may also have gotten large enough so that it will be difficult to train them up the stakes. Tomato plants are not natural climbers like peas and beans, so they must be tied to the stakes as they grow. The purpose of the stakes is to keep the plants off the ground and away from slugs and dampness, and to facilitate harvesting the tomatoes when they're ripe. Stakes should be at least an inch in diameter to accommodate the weight of the plants, and should be set so that about four feet of stake is aboveground.

Once the plants are established, don't feed them high-nitrogen fertilizer, because excessive nitrogen will encourage leafy growth rather than fruit. A midseason application of high-phosphate fertilizer is all the feeding they will need.

Water tomato plants deeply once a week. If they are allowed to go for too long without water and then watered copiously, the sudden influx of water may cause the tomatoes to swell so suddenly that their skins will split.

Some gardeners prune their plants, removing all the non-bearing branches to direct the plant's energy to the fruit. This may also have some advantage in that it allows for better air circulation and more sunlight reaching the tomatoes themselves. It is also a good practice to remove new growth that forms after the first of August; blooms set that late in the season won't have time to mature anyway, and there is no point in letting the plant waste its energy on them.

Most of the problems of pests on tomato plants occur when the plants are very young. Leaf-eating insects should be controlled with rotenone. During cool, wet summers a fungus disease called tomato blight may cause plants to turn black and die; the only remedy for this disease is to remove affected plants and burn them to keep the disease from spreading.

Before the first frost in the fall, tomato plants should be pulled up and hung upside down in a garage or other protected place. Stored in this way, the remaining fruit will ripen nicely. Tomatoes can also be picked from the vine and set out on trays or newspapers to ripen.

TURNIPS: An easy, fast crop that provides both greens and roots, turnips can be planted in the early spring, or at any time during the growing season. A crop planted in the fall will mature the following spring, just when garden produce is at a premium.

An entire package of turnip seeds is generally too many to plant at once, but succession sowings can be made at two-week intervals if you'd like a steady supply.

Plant turnips any time after the first of March. Thin seedlings to stand five inches apart. The thinnings can be used in the kitchen or added to the compost pile. When plants are well established, a few leaves from each plant can be picked for use as greens.

Harvest turnips when they are still young and sweet; if left in the ground too long they will become woody and slightly bitter.

Slugs may take their share of the foliage, and leaf-eating insects may cause problems when the plants are young. And an occasional root maggot may make a meal on the turnips themselves. The leaf-eaters can be controlled with rotenone, and the root maggots with Diazinon or wood ashes worked into the soil. Serious insect problems with turnips are the exception rather than the rule, though. Most insects, given a choice in the matter, would prefer some of your other, more tender crops, and will eat turnips only if they're really hungry.

Appendix

Help!

GOVERNMENT ASSISTANCE

Government agencies in Oregon, Washington, and British Columbia provide soil tests for $5.00 to home gardeners, and will diagnose insect problems and plant diseases. Always inquire first about what sort of sample to send them before you mail them bugs or dirt. For soil samples, the agencies provide special containers and directions on how to collect samples; for insects and diseases they can advise you by phone what sort of sample they'll need.

British Columbia

Victoria	B.C. Ministry of Agriculture Soils Department (for soil tests) Plant Pathology and Entomology (for pests & diseases) 808 Douglas Victoria, B.C. V8W 2Z7 Phone 387-5121
Abbotsford	B.C. Ministry of Agriculture 33780 Laurel Street Abbotsford, B.C. V2S IX4 Phone 859-5281

Cloverdale   B.C. Ministry of Agriculture
Box 1172
Station A, Surrey
Cloverdale, B.C.
Phone 576-2911

Washington Cooperative Extension Services

Clallam County   166 W. Eighth St.
Port Angeles, Washington 98362
Phone 452-2371

Clark County   Box 5000
Vancouver, Washington 98660
Phone 699-2385

Cowlitz County   Courthouse Annex
Kelso, Washington 98626
Phone 577-3014

Grays Harbor County Courthouse, Box 552
Montesano, Washington 98563
Phone 249-4332

Island County   Courthouse
Coupeville, Washington 98239
Phone 678-5111 ext. 263

Jefferson County   Federal Bldg., Box 572
Port Townsend, Washington 98368
Phone 385-3581

King County   King County Courthouse, E531
Seattle, Washington 98104
Phone 344-2686

Kitsap County   Courthouse Annex, Box 146
Port Orchard, Washington 98366
Phone 876-7157

Lewis County — Courthouse Annex
Chehalis, Washington 98532
Phone 748-8603

Mason County — 12 Federal Bldg.
Shelton, Washington 98584
Phone 426-4732

Pacific County — Courthouse, Box 88
South Bend, Washington 98586
Phone 875-5031

Pierce County — 5601 Sixth Avenue
Tacoma, Washington 98406
Phone 593-4190

San Juan County — Schuman Bldg.
Friday Harbor, Washington 98250
Phone 378-4414

Skagit County — 306 Courthouse
Mt. Vernon, Washington 98273
Phone 336-9322

Snohomish County — Agriculture Bldg.
Everett, Washington 98201
Phone 259-9422

Thurston County — 226 Courthouse Annex
Olympia, Washington 98501
Phone 753-8056

Wahkiakum County — Courthouse, Box 278
Cathlamet, Washington 98612
Phone 795-3661

Whatcom County — Courthouse Annex
1000 N. Forest Street
Bellingham, Washington 98225
Phone 676-6736

Oregon Cooperative Extension Services

Benton County   Post Office Box B
Corvallis, Oregon 97330
Phone 752-7186

Clackamas County   256 Warner-Milne Road
Oregon City, Oregon 97045
Phone 655-8631

Clatsop County   Post Office Box 207
Astoria, Oregon 97103
Phone 325-7441, Ext. 50

Columbia County   Courthouse
St. Helens, Oregon 97051
Phone 397-3462

Coos County   Courthouse
Coquille, Oregon 97423
Phone 396-3121, Ext. 246

Curry County   County Office Bldg.
P.O. Box 488
Gold Beach, Oregon 97444
Phone 247-7011, Ext. 226

Douglas County   1134 S.E. Douglas Avenue
P.O. Box 1165
Roseburg, Oregon 97470
Phone 672-4461

Hood River   Courthouse, P.O. Box 499
Hood River, Oregon 97031
Phone 386-3343

Josephine County   215 Ringuette St.
Grants Pass, Oregon 97526
Phone 476-6613

Lane County	950 W. 13th Street P.O. Box 2308 Eugene, Oregon 97402 Phone 687-4243
Lincoln County	Courthouse, 225 W. Olive Street Newport, Oregon 97365 Phone 265-5376
Linn County	Courthouse Annex, P.O. Box 765 Albany, Oregon 97321 Phone 928-9323
Marion County	3180 Center Street N.E., Room 160 Salem, Oregon 97301 Phone 588-5301
Multnomah County	1633 S.W. Park P.O. Box 1261 Portland, Oregon 97207 Phone 229-4830 North Willamette Area Extension Office Ross Island Center 049 S.W. Porter Portland, Oregon 97201
Polk County	Room 104, Courthouse Dallas, Oregon 97338 Phone 623-8171, Ext. 56
Tillamook County	Courthouse Tillamook, Oregon 97141 Phone 842-5511, Ext. 372
Washington County	Branch Co. Office Bldg., Courthouse Hillsboro, Oregon 97123 Phone 648-8771

Yamhill County   Room 42, Courthouse
McMinnville, Oregon 97128
Phone 472-9371, Ext. 251

SEED CATALOGUES

The following is only a sampling of the multitude of available seed catalogues. If this isn't enough for you, pick up the December issue of any gardening magazine, and you will find advertisements for many more. Those below are all free; some of the others require a small fee.

Nichols Herbs and Rare Seeds
Nichols Garden Nursery
1190 North Pacific Hwy.
Albany, Oregon 97321

Thompson and Morgan Inc.
P.O. Box 24, 401 Kennedy Blvd.
Somerdale, New Jersey 08083

Henry Field Seed & Nursery Co.
Shenandoah, Iowa 51602

The Natural Development Co.
Box 215
Bainbridge, Pennsylvania 17502

Seedway, Inc.
Hall, New York 14463

George W. Park Seed Co., Inc.
P.O. Box 31
Greenwood, South Carolina 29647

Jackson & Perkins Co.
Medford, Oregon 97501

Stokes Seeds Ltd.
Box 10
St. Catharines, Ontario
L4R 6R6

Dominion Seed House
Georgetown, Ontario
L7G 4A2

McKenzie, Steele Briggs Seed Co.
Box 1060
Brandon, Manitoba
R7A 6E1

Island Seed Co.
Box 4278, Sta. A
Victoria, B.C.
V8X 3X8

Index

Index